ST★RS WITHOUT G★RTERS!

Authors' royalties from this edition of *Stars Without Garters!* will be paid directly to Broadway Cares/Equity Fights AIDS.

ST★RS WITHOUT G★RTERS!

The Memoirs of
Two Gay GIs in WWII

by C. Tyler Carpenter
& Edward H. Yeatts

Alamo Square Press
San Francisco

Copyright © 1996 by C. Tyler Carpenter & Edward H. Yeatts

All rights reserved. Printed in the United States of America. No part of this book may be used or reproduced in any manner whatsoever without written permission except in the case of brief quotations embodied in critical articles or reviews. For information, address Alamo Square Press, P.O. Box 14543, San Francisco, CA 94114.

Library of Congress Cataloging-in-Publication Data

Carpenter, C. Tyler, 1915–
    Stars without garters!: the memoirs of two gay GIs in World War II / by C. Tyler Carpenter & Edward H. Yeatts.
        p.   cm.
    ISBN: 1-886360-03-0 (alk. paper). — ISBN: 1-886360-04-9 (paper: alk. paper)
    1. Carpenter, C. Tyler, 1915–   . 2. Fuller, Edward Gray, d. 1979. 3. World War, 1939–1945—Personal narratives, American. 4. United States. Army—Biography. 5. United States. Army, Service Unit, 1209th—History. 6. United States—Armed Forces—Gays—Biography.
I. Yeatts, Edward H., 1936–   . II. Title.
D811.5.C285   1996   96-13649
940.54´7—dc20   CIP

Readers should not make assumption or inference about the sexual orientation of any person identified in the text unless that preference is clearly stated by the authors. In some cases, names have been modified to protect the privacy of individuals and their families.

10   9   8   7   6   5   4   3   2   1

DEDICATION

In loving memory of Edward Grey Fuller and the soldiers in the 1209th CASU, the 78th Lightning Division and the 34th Special Service Company who used their talents to soothe the sting of war for millions and, subsequently, helped to save the world.

ACKNOWLEDGMENTS

Thousands of books about World War II have been published since the Allied Forces triumphed over the Axis Nations in 1945, but few celebrate the patriotic service of gays and lesbians in the most significant event of the century. This volume is my contribution to the small, but growing, collection of history which focuses on homosexuals in the military.

This book would not exist without the friendship, wisdom and patience of Charles Tyler Carpenter. Mutual friends introduced me to Ty and Eddie Fuller in 1960. Through the years each of them told me various anecdotes of their shared military service. In 1980 I asked Ty to make all-inclusive tapes of their fascinating true story. Ty gave me his army career which allowed me to realize my lifelong ambition to write an important book. During the next decade I searched for, located and examined primary sources until I was able to reconstruct and document all of the major events of their participation in World War II. And by this effort, I finally came to understand the significant era of my childhood. Thanks, Ty, for making me a bigger man, too.

For their assistance with research, I am grateful to the librarians and staff of the National Archives and Record Service, the United States Military Center of History, the Fort Drum Historical Museum, the George C. Marshall Library, the University of Virginia Alderman Library, the Jones Memorial Library and the Museum of Broadcasting.

Phillip Dickinson, author of "Odyssey of the 34th" (1945), deserves special recognition. His unpublished monograph was an invaluable supplement to the official military records.

I thank Allan Berubé and the staff of the Gay and Lesbian Historical Society of Northern California for providing copies of many primary sources.

I offer eternal devotion to my esteemed students Jason Berkley, Barrett Bryant, Brandyn Chapman, Andy Cowgill, Erika Elder, Jud Howell, Chris Markham, Steve MacDonald, Jay White and Stacy Williamson—National History Day finalists and Virginia History Day champions in 1986, 1987 and 1988—who supplemented my research and inspired me to do my best.

For their valuable advice and encouragement, I express gratitude to Jane C. Andes, Geoffrey R. Cates (U.S. Navy), William E. Calohan III, Dick Leitsch, Judy B. Martin, John K. Pepper, Jr., Larry D. Powell (U.S. Air Force), Margaret H. Ritter and E. William Wright (U.S. Army).

It is indeed a priviledge to thank the many veterans and civilians—straight and gay—who discussed the WW II years, answered letters and/or loaned cherished documents such as scrapbooks, letters, citations and photographs: Linda Jo Barr (U.S. Navy), Marjory J. Bassett, Cliff Bell (U.S. Army), Martha W.

Bing, Estelle C. Bird (Red Cross), Richard K. Bleser (U.S. Army), Louise Brown, Mickey Brooks (U.S. Navy), John R. Bucklin (U.S. Army), Elizabeth Caldwell, Calvin Candler, Emilee Hines Cantieri, Richard B. Carpenter, Linda B. Ceresole (Red Cross), Madolin S. Cervantes (U.S. Army), Charles Chevillot (French Resistance), Tom Collier (U.S. Army Air Corps), William J. Crane (U.S. Army), Kenneth Crouch, Nancy Jane Cushman (USO), Mabel Davidson (Red Cross), Harold J. DeArmona, Herbert Dube (U.S. Army), Nellie I. Feagans (U.S. Army), Maxine M. Fleanor, Wallace Fox (U.S. Army), Marianna H. Fox, Mike and Marinel Fuller, Lilo Geiger, Manne Gottlieb (U.S. Army), William R. Guill (U.S. Army), Bill Hall (U.S. Navy), Hunter Hale, Shelby Hinckle (USO), Robert Hon (U.S. Army), Edward Houstoun (U.S. Navy), Mabel C. Houstoun, Partick Houstoun, John Hurt (U.S. Navy), Franklin Kerr (U.S. Navy), Dorothy and Virginia Lanier, Ronald E. Letch (British Army), Therese LeVesque (U.S. Marine Corps), Raymond E. Lipscomb (U.S. Army), Louis MacDonald (USO), Bobby MacMillian (U.S. Army—Bataan Death March Survivor), Wilbert B. Mahoney (U.S. Army), Eddie Malenowski (U.S. Army), E. Anne Mallet (USO), Alfred Marggraf (U.S. Army), Evan Marshall (U.S. Army), Marcella C. Marshall, Matt Mattingly (U.S. Army), Robert J. McKenzie (U.S. Army), Bill Merriken (U.S. Army), Minnie T. Miles, Mr. and Mrs. E. Ray Nance (U.S. Army), Brenda Noel, William Overstreet (U.S. Navy), Paul J. Palcsak (U.S. Navy), Georgiana H. Pope, Jo-Ellen Porter, Nellie F. Powell, Theodore J. Ritter (U.S. Navy), Gordan Roach (British Army), Lester Robertson (U.S. Army), Alfred V. Ross (U.S. Army Air Corps), Vincent E. Ross, Don Ruzek (U.S. Navy), Bernard Saunders (U.S. Army Air Corps—Bataan Death March survivor), James Scarborough (U.S. Army), Kermit Schafer (U.S. Army), Bernd G. Schmidt (German Army), Jerome Shane (U.S. Army), Chauncey E. Spencer (U.S. Army Air Corps), Don Stamper, Miriam Stovall, Richard Stretz (U.S. Navy), Jeri Talbott (USO), Jane S. Tedder, Louise Terrell, Gertrude Thaxton, William C. Tinsley (U.S. Army), John Turner (U.S. Army), Herbert W. Tweedy (U.S. Army), J. Thornton Tweedy (U.S. Army), Robert N. Waggoner (U.S. Army), George Wayland (U.S. Navy), Max Weatherly, Jack Welles (U.S. Army), Hugo J. Winkler (German Army), Lutie B. Wright, Margaret Woodford (U.S. Army) and Margaret T. Yeatts.

I thank Skip Mooney and the entire staff at Broadway Cares/Equity Fights AIDS and, indeed, all the AIDS support organizations for their very important work.

Finally, I am indebted beyond words to my publisher Bert Herrman for his enthusiasm and guidance. He made my ambition a reality.

Edward H. Yeatts
Miami, Florida, October, 1995

PROLOGUE

"Wake up, honey boy. Four a.m. Time to get ready."

May 9, 1941. I was scheduled to report to the induction center to be drafted into the United States Army in two hours. "Oh, Eddie. I can't face it. I don't want to join the army. I don't want to leave you."

"You'll be fine, Tyler," Eddie assured me, "the best and handsomest soldier in the whole army."

We rode the subway downtown to the New York City armory on 34th Street. Lengthy lines of soon-to-be soldiers waited. The guys maintained a brave facade while weeping girls clung onto them. Eddie and I brushed shoulders and looked at each other. We were in a closet forced on us by the civility of government and the charity of organized religion.

Finally, it was time to enter. The boys and girls kissed. Eddie and I shook hands, a convention that fell far short of the embrace and kiss we both wanted and deserved. "Tyler, you'll be fine. You can do anything that any of the other guys can do," Eddie said. I breathed deep, climbed the steps and entered an unknown world.

I passed dozens of physical tests and the psychiatrist's "Do-you-like-girls?" routine. After five hours of pokes and probes, hundreds of us recited the Pledge of Allegiance and officially became privates in the United States Army. Mid-afternoon, we hiked to Penn Station and boarded trains for Fort Dix, New Jersey. Thousands of relatives, girlfriends and Eddie—awash in tears—waved and yelled good-byes from behind the barricades.

Neither Eddie nor I realized that we were beginning the greatest adventure of our lives.

At Fort Dix we were assigned quarters and fed. I liked the army chow. I reasoned that if I were going to be miserable, at least I could ease the pain with a full stomach. In the barracks, the men speculated about where we might be shipped for basic training and named exotic locales. I shuddered when California was mentioned. Sweet Jesus, if the army stationed me on the West Coast, I wouldn't see Eddie for a year.

The guy in the next bunk—Walter Nichols, a gregarious kid from Patterson, New Jersey—and I talked. He showed me a photograph of his girlfriend and pictures of his family. I showed him pictures of Derby Rogers, "my girl," and snapshots of my widowed mother and five brothers. I even showed him a picture of Eddie Fuller, "my best pal." That night I prayed. "Please, dear Lord, don't let them ship me thousands of miles away. Please let me be posted near home."

For three days, we spent endless hours in endless lines. It was my initiation to "hurry up and wait," the army's way. We tolerated additional medical tests, dental exams and ugly haircuts. We learned to stand reveille and retreat, plus a few simple facings. Finally, we received general issue clothing, and at last we looked liked GIs. I ached for Eddie and home.

CHAPTER 1

"As soon as you guys finish setups for tomorrow, you can go," said Pat, the restaurant owner. "The radio says that 12 to 18 inches of snow are expected by daybreak. No more customers tonight."

I had served only one party since the theatres let out. Betty Hutton, the pretty and pert ingenue, and several of the Gypsies in *Panama Hattie* playing at the 46th Street Theatre behind our building braved the elements through the alley, but they ate quickly and left. The other waiters and I rushed and were ready to leave by midnight. I delighted in the first snowfall of winter on December 11, 1940.

I moved to New York City from Jacksonville, Florida in October 1938. Like millions of aspiring performers before and since, I made rounds, went to auditions and worked as a waiter. With six seasons of stock and repertory to my credit, I felt prepared for my chosen vocation. But in many respects I was a rube, and I brooded over my prodigious secret. I was a 23-year-old, sexually ambivalent virgin.

Theatrical employment eluded me until the spring of 1939, when I was hired for a ten-week summer stock season in Lake Mohopac, New York. I earned five dollars a week plus room and board. Edward, my 15-year-old brother, spent the season with me. He did odd jobs at the theatre for room, meals and tips.

When I returned to Manhattan in September, I landed a supporting role as a college student in a Broadway flop, *Where Do We Go From Here?* I got a few radio jobs during the winter. Then in the spring of 1940, I joined the cast of *Billy Rose's Aquacade* in its second season at the New York World's Fair. As a swimmer/dancer I earned the stupendous salary of 36 dollars a week for a 20-week engagement.

Olympic swimmers Buster Crabbe, Eleanor Holm and Gertrude Ederle were the Aquacade headliners, plus Stubby Kaye and the Vincent Lopez Orchestra. We played to packed houses at the 15,000-seat amphitheater in Flushing Meadow on Lake Success—four performances a day, seven days a week. The schedule was taxing, but I relished every moment. The chorus elected me cast representative to the newly formed union, AGVA—American Guild of Variety Artists.

During that summer, almost every conversation included some reference to the war in Europe. The newspaper and radio reports of the Battle of Britain and Occupied Paris alarmed everyone. Public opinion regarding America's entry into the war gradually changed from negative to reluctant resignation. Even though Congress remained isolationist, many citizens realized that Nazi aggression would have to be thwarted. When people talked about "The War," they seldom mentioned the fighting in Asia. Congress passed the Selective Service Act in September, and I was one of the 16,313,240 men who registered and received a draft card in October.

I gleefully trekked along the snow-covered, deserted streets. On the southeast corner of Sixth Avenue and 53rd Street, I met a young man going in the opposite direction. We glanced at each other, as in "cruising," and I swear I heard bells ring. I pivoted and saw that he had crossed the street. He stood facing me from the northeast corner. He looked incredibly handsome standing there in his snow-flecked Chesterfield. I strolled toward Fifth Avenue, and he strolled in the same direction directly across the street. I stopped by a fence, and he stopped in a doorway. We stood motionless and stared at each other through the swirling snow. Rivulets of sweat rolled down my rib cage. My heartbeat accelerated. I wanted to dash across the street, but I felt paralyzed. Finally, just when I found the courage to approach him, he walked across to me.

"Do you have a match?" His voice was masculine and melodious.

"Oh, yes. Yes, I do," I stammered.

"Would you like a cigarette?"

"No, thanks. I hate to smoke outdoors in the snow." I instantly regretted my stupid reply. I regained my wits and blurted out, "Can we go for coffee?" I struck the match and the flame illuminated his princely face.

"I know just the place," he said. "Let's hustle before we're buried in an avalanche." We made inane conversation about the projected snowfall while we trudged to a cafeteria near 55th Street. He purchased two coffees. Once we discovered that we were both actors, the conversation flowed. Twenty minutes later, he invited me to his apartment for a drink.

He chased his sleeping roommate off the sofa and into the bedroom.

He served hot-buttered rum. He told me about growing up in Missouri. He emphasized his fondness for basketball and told me about his college days in Springfield. The depression had forced him to leave the University at the end of his sophomore year, so he'd come to New York in 1933 to conquer Broadway. He said he hadn't exactly set the theatrical world on fire, but he had racked up some decent credits. After he received good notices for his performance in *Whatever Possessed Her*, he received a scholarship to the National Shakespeare Theatre in England in 1935. "That's when I really found out what it means to be an actor," he said. "Of the six shows I've done on Broadway, my favorite was *The Cradle Will Rock* directed by Orson Welles. I don't sing or dance worth a hoot, but Marc Blitzstein wanted only natural voices for his controversial opera."

I told him that when I appeared on radio with Will Geer, Will had explained to me that the protests and riots in and around the theatre during the run of *Cradle* were memorable events. My new friend said Will was a terrific actor and asked what show I had done with him. "NBC's *Gallant American Women*. Mrs. Roosevelt was the guest."

"That's a real honor. Mrs. Roosevelt is a class act."

I told him about growing up in Florida. I emphasized my fondness for swimming and volleyball. I shared details on my theatrical credits and felt inadequate. The third lead in a quick flop and a chorus job didn't compare. After we covered sports and careers, we swapped family stories. I inserted whatever I could to brighten up my past. Edward Grey Fuller at 29 was sophisticated, intelligent and successful; everything I wanted to be, but feared I never would.

While we talked and drank, we subtly flirted and created opportunities for lots of incidental touching. He told me about a discreet New York Society of gay professionals. He exposed me to the real world. Eventually he kissed me and opened my fly to expose my erection, which had been insistent for what seemed an eternity. It was back to the sofa for the roommate, while we discovered bliss in the bedroom. He was gentle. I exploded. Together we soared.

When I left at daylight, I knew I had found my life's companion. The cold wind and the deep snow did not daunt the springtime in my heart. I was in love.

I shared an apartment on East 52nd Street with a platonic friend, Scott Griffin. We had been members of the same stock company in Florida. I suppressed my urge to awaken Scott and tell him about the monumental event of my life. He might not appreciate or sanction a liaison between men.

At noon our buzzer rang. When I answered, Eddie's voice serenaded me through the intercom. He opened the conversation by saying that he wanted to make certain I felt all right about the events of the previous evening. After Scott left for work, Eddie and I picked up where we had left off that morning; lots of passionate kisses and erotic massage. Our tongues and hands went everywhere at once! We could not get enough of each other.

CHAPTER 2

Eddie and I became a steady item. Robert Haig, my best friend, sensed the change in me. Bob, a music and theatre critic, often took me to the opera and ballet which I could never have afforded. After I refused several invitations, he asked what the matter was. I told Bob the truth.

"Damn you, Tyler. Don't you know I'm in love with you?" Bob asked. I was shocked. Bob said that he had been courting me for almost a year. "What did you think, or did you think at all?"

"Honestly, Bob, I didn't think anything. I thought we were friends."

"I've been waiting months for you to discover your sexual self. Move in with me," he demanded. "I love you. I know I can make you happy."

"Bob, don't you see? I'm in love with Eddie Fuller. You're my friend and a darned good one, but I'm not in love with you."

He stood and flung his napkin on the table. "Oh, shit! Queens." He stormed out of the restaurant.

By the second week of 1941, Eddie and I decided we must live together. So Eddie moved in with me and Scott, who was glad to have a third person to share the rent. I was merry as a cricket after Eddie moved in at 22 East 52nd Street. Even bathing became an intoxicating event. Fortunately, the tub was large enough to accommodate two six-foot-two males anxious to blow bubbles. We lived directly across from the world-famous 21 Club. Three doors east at Tony's, a sophisticated bar and dining room, jazz-stylist Mabel Mercer performed nightly. Jackie Gleason, a sparkling new comic, emceed at the popular Club 18 in the basement of our building. We lived on "Swing Street" and we swung with and on each other. Every morning until 4:00 a.m. we could hear and feel the pulsating rhythms from below, but it didn't bother us. We were young and in love and together. Dear Scott, in his bed with his face to the wall, never complained about the music or the noises Eddie and I made in the throes of carnal ecstasy.

Before I met Eddie, I adamantly rejected socializing with homosexuals. All my life I had been brainwashed by my family and peers to believe that queers were unnatural and dirty; consequently, I hated myself for the unnatural and dirty feelings I had harbored since the age of five. For years I feared that I would do or say something that would expose me as being one of "them." Eddie's respect for and understanding of my insecurity nourished our love. Eddie wasn't unnatural and dirty. He was a wonderful, handsome man, and he loved me.

Eddie introduced me to his many friends. We went to cocktail parties and dinners with delightful gays, lesbians and straights. Jerry Reimers, an executive with the telephone company, and his lover took Eddie and me as their guests to see Gertrude Lawrence in the spectacular Kurt Weill musical, *Lady In The Dark*. Danny Kaye, Lucille Bremer and Victor Mature—each destined for movie stardom—were featured. Eddie took us backstage to meet Miss Lawrence. She greeted us cordially because we were Eddie's friends. I was so proud to be Eddie's companion; wherever we went people were always genuinely pleased to see him.

An important part of my coming-out education occurred in gay bars. We frequented The Dizzy Club on 52nd Street two blocks west of our apartment. Stephen, a bartender, and Eddie had appeared together on Broadway. College boys, young professionals and hunky blue-collar types camped and danced to the Dizzy's ear-splitting jukebox. Harold Norse called it "an orgy room for the fully clad...a writhing mass of tight boys in tighter pants." The street-level bar in the Astor Hotel on Broadway at 44th Street was a discreet watering hole where everyone could make contact. The Pink Elephant at 42nd and Sixth was a hustler bar. Shelton Corner, the 123 Club and Cerutti's—where Bricktop, chanteuse and friend of the great and near-great, was hostess—were other bars we patronized, but the Golden Pheasant on East 56th Street was a favorite because it catered to gay showfolk. The jukebox constantly serenaded us with Dinah Shore's swinging rendition of "My Heart Belongs To Daddy" and "Beethoven's Fifth Symphony," affectionately called "Mary Astor's Piece" by fans of the Bette Davis film, *The Great Lie*. We conformed to the gay-uniform dress code—business suits, wide ties and fedora hats—and we tried our damnedest to appear suave, dapper and butch like film idols Tyrone Power, Randolph Scott and Joel McCrea.

I soon discovered that homosexuals were just like the general population: male, female, single, married, young, old, fat, thin, black, white, Asian, rich, smart, handsome, ugly and every other adjective that describes the human condition. A great democratic fraternity!

CHAPTER 3

"Hors d'oeuvres, anyone?" asked the perky girl in the mink coat and matching peekaboo hat. She gently tugged on Eddie's earlobe and voila, an egg. She flashed a dazzling ingenue smile. "How about you, Mr. C.?" She reached into my pocket and presto, another egg. "Sausages?" From her coat sleeve, she retrieved a string of fake Italian franks. "Sorry, darlings. They aren't edible," she mused, "but if you're free on Thursday, I'll prepare you a non-theatrical dinner. Real food, just like at the Automat."

"Derby, honey," Eddie sputtered between convulsive giggles, "you're a hoot. We'd love to dine with you anytime, any place."

"Ty, are you impressed by my powers of prestidigitation?" she queried.

"I'm fascinated. Where did you come by such extraordinary talents?"

"I'm studying magic," she responded. "If I can't make it on Broadway as a legitimate actress, I want to join the circus or maybe do a nightclub act. I'm studying voice and dance just in case." She raised her hand and spoke into an imaginary megaphone. "For the benefit of any talent scouts present, I wish to make an impudent declaration. I'm an expert horse woman. I cook and sew. I play bridge, backgammon and Chinese checkers, but I vacuum or iron only when absolutely forced to." Eddie was in stitches and I was captivated. Between sips of her cocktail Derby sighed, "As Mr. Hemingway so aptly remarked, 'Martinis make me feel civilized.'"

Elizabeth Laura Derby Rogers beamed like summer sunshine that bleak January afternoon when Eddie introduced us at the Taft Hotel Bar. Eddie had met Derby at the American Academy of Dramatic Arts, where she was a second-year student. She was beautiful, vivacious and intelligent—a younger, prettier and funnier version of the screw-ball comedy heroines played in the movies by Irene Dunne, Carole Lombard and Jean Arthur—and I adored her on sight. Derby and her family lived at the Prince George Hotel on East 28th Street just off Fifth Avenue. It was the last of seven hotels built, owned and operated by her father. Her mother Helen welcomed Derby's poverty-stricken, theatrical friends, and they often invited us to dinner. I quickly became Derby's favorite bridge partner, and we often went on dates to the theatre or dancing, with and without Eddie.

Eddie had a girlfriend, too. Actress Edie Groome was a bubbly, attractive blonde with immense brown eyes. She and Eddie appeared together in Federal Theatre productions of *The Torchbearers* and *The Bat*. Edie was unconditionally in love with Eddie. Through the years, they developed a loving and sexual friendship. When he explained his entire make-up, she accepted it. Edie was an unusual young woman. When I came on the scene, she embraced me as if it were the most natural thing in the world. "I'm so happy that Eddie has found someone to share his life. And I'm happy for you, too." Then she kissed me.

Derby filled a real need in my life. I had a girlfriend to introduce to my family and heterosexual friends. One warm April evening after many martinis, Derby announced that she was in love with me. I loved her, too, but serious boy-girl romance was not for me. I had just come to grips with my homosexuality. I didn't know how to respond to Derby's amorous overtures. I wanted to tell her that I was in love with Eddie, but I wasn't prepared to admit I was gay for fear I would lose her friendship. I felt saddened and guilty. As soon as I got home, I explained the situation to Eddie. "I always knew Derby had excellent taste," Eddie responded.

"Aw, go on," I said. "Seriously, what should I do?"

"Of course, she's in love with you. She's a normal, healthy 21-year-old female, and she's hot for you because you're the best-looking and most fun-loving man she's ever met," Eddie said. "She loves you for the same reasons I do."

"That doesn't answer my question."

"Baby, I can't presume to advise you," Eddie replied. "It's your decision. Just don't do anything rash. I'm sure you'll sort it out."

To the public, Eddie and I appeared as fellow actors and good friends who dated girls, but we were happiest together in the gay world among our own. Together our closets became a grand ballroom. We led double lives, and we enjoyed both.

Since being in love with either man or woman is not a career, we searched for theatrical employment during the early months of 1941. Eddie got the occasional radio job. Edie wrote radio commercials for an agency. Derby did showcases at the Academy. I picked up modeling jobs at *True Detective* and *My True Story* magazines posing in various guises—the lover, the chauffeur and the killer—with lots of sexy girls.

Life was good and I was happy, until the day I received the green letter of "Greetings" from President Roosevelt. "Damn it, I don't understand. Why me? I'm the only person I know who's gotten a draft notice," I ranted.

"Well, there are options," Eddie responded between tears. "You can declare your homosexuality, and you'll automatically be disqualified from service."

"Never," I retorted. "I may be as queer as Oscar Wilde, but I'm a man. I won't give the bigots the satisfaction of saying that the sissy didn't serve his country."

"Good for you, baby. You show 'em."

I rationalized I would be in the army for just one year as the government promised, and then I could return to my idyllic civilian life. However, I feared it might be longer. As the fighting on both sides of the world escalated, America's ability to remain neutral appeared doubtful. "Whatever happens, we'll manage," Eddie assured me.

"It solves the dilemma of what to tell Derby," I said. "I won't have to tell her anything at least for a year."

In preparation for my departure, Eddie and I embarked on a two-week orgy of revelry and sex. Derby hosted several farewell dinners. Bob Haig, Jerry Reimers and other friends staged bon-voyage soirees. And we hit the bars every night. Sandwiched between our public celebrations were private celebrations in bed and in the oversized bathtub. Since I had discovered sex-without-guilt as my favorite indoor sport, I made up for many years of denial. It was a splendid time until the dreaded morning of May 9, 1941 when Eddie said, "Wake up, honey boy. Four a.m. Time to get ready."

CHAPTER 4

"Where in hell is Jefferson Barracks?"
"Just outside St. Louis."
"Hot damn, I'm going to Fort Oglethorpe."
"Ditto, buddy. I heard wild stories about them Georgia peaches."
"Ty," Walt Nichols shouted above the din of hundreds naming their assignments, "where are you headed?"
"Pine Camp, New York," I shouted back.
"Yahoo, me too," Walt yelled and gave the okay sign. "Close to home."

Pine Camp, 28 miles south of the Canadian border near Watertown was a mere seven hours by car or train from Manhattan. My prayers were answered. I joined the 4th Armored Division, Company C of the 24th Engineers Battalion. Walt was assigned to the post motor pool so I seldom saw him during basic training which lasted 11 weeks. I dedicated all my attention to learning the ropes and gave each activity my best effort. I remembered what Eddie had said, "You'll be the best soldier in the whole army." I had to be successful. I was gay.

Engineering units were responsible for making thousands of acres ready for field training. My platoon built roads and bridges. It was my first experience at heavy manual labor. I operated rock crushers, laid railroad ties and felled trees. For this unique employment I earned 21 dollars a month. In a few weeks I was in great physical shape. I gained 15 solid pounds and felt terrific, but I was so homesick.

Several times a week, Eddie wrote long, loving letters which I kept in my footlocker for multiple readings to confirm I had a life outside the army. Derby wrote almost every day. She was my pin-up girl and I plastered her pictures all over my footlocker. The guys were impressed; they called her "Ty's 'real-live' actress girlfriend."

I made corporal in six weeks. The company commander promoted me after he heard my speech congratulating our 1st Sergeant who made OCS (officers candidate school). As squad leader—the equivalent of a drill sergeant—I taught troops the nomenclature and operation of M-1 and Springfield rifles, machine guns and small cannons. I taught the men to use explosives, and I supervised obstacle course construction. Most of the men seemed to like me, but I had not made a close buddy.

More than half of the men in my outfit couldn't swim. Almost as many didn't read and write well enough to maintain contact with their loved ones. (In 1941, telephones in private homes were a luxury item.) Most of the boys from large cities didn't know how to drive a car so they couldn't operate army vehicles. A group of us were assigned to instruct those basic skills.

Private Anthony LaPolla, a fellow instructor with a 167 IQ, had a winning smile and a charismatic personality. When I observed the 20-year-old, stocky Italian-American from Bayonne teaching the guys to swim and drive, I saw that he was a compassionate man. He displayed the patience of Job when he helped the men write letters and read their replies. I decided to cultivate Tony's friendship. As captain of the squad's volleyball team, I persuaded Tony to join us. At 5'7", he was the shortest man on the team, but he was an expert athlete—a 1939 Golden Gloves champ—and played like a much taller man. Big Band singer Helen O'Connell's rendition of "Amapola" was a hit parade leader that summer. One afternoon when the team was celebrating a victory with many beers in the PX, I put my arm around Tony's shoulder and sang, "LaPolla, our winning little Poppy..." The guys laughed, and the tag stuck. Poppy liked his nickname. At last I had a buddy.

Eddie's letters were a source of comfort and discomfort. If they fell into the wrong hands, it would mean serious trouble. I decided to take the letters into the woods and burn them. I invited Poppy to go with me on a personal errand. We walked a good distance from the barracks to a cleared area. We sat on stumps. "Poppy, I asked you to come out here with me because there's something you should know if we're going to remain friends." I took a deep breath. Then I just blurted out, "I'm a homosexual."

Poppy listened attentively while I told him about Eddie. I told him about Derby, Edie and Bob Haig. I read portions of Eddie's letters. I ended my monologue, "Do you have any questions?"

Poppy stood and walked to me with an extended hand. He clasped my hand. "No, I'm satisfied, but I'll need some time to process it." He lit a cigarette and waited while I burned Eddie's letters.

During the stroll back to the barracks, we discussed baseball. Poppy raved about his beloved Yankees and Joe DiMaggio's sensational season. I teased him that the Dodgers might drub his Yankees in the next World Series.

"Hey, Ty, did you hear the one about the Italian immigrant who went to his first baseball game?" I shook my head no. "Well, this guy just over from the old country went with his American cousin to Yankee Stadium. When he found out that DiMaggio was Italian, the guy went ape. Joe got a single his first trip to the plate. The immigrant yelled, 'Run-a Joe. Run-a Joe.' Joe hit a triple his next time up. The guy shouted, 'Run-a Joe. Run-a Joe.' On his third plate appearance, DiMaggio walked. The guy shouted, 'Run-a Joe, run-a Joe' until his cousin explained that DiMaggio was walking because he got four balls. The immigrant beamed. Then he yelled, 'Walk-a proud, Joe, walk-a proud!'"

The next afternoon following a volleyball game, Poppy slapped me on the back and said, "Thanks, Ty, for making me a bigger man."

The magazines I posed for in February hit the PX newsstands in July. One of the guys spotted my picture. Several of the men bought copies and tacked pictures of me with sexy girls all around the barracks including the latrine. I was flattered. The men elevated me to celebrity status. I didn't spoil their excitement by telling them that the jobs actually meant financial survival for a struggling actor and his male lover. The dear innocents would never have understood. Only Poppy.

CHAPTER 5

Eddie's smile was wider than the Grand Canyon on July 26 when he stepped off the train in Watertown followed by Derby and Helen Rogers.

"You look wonderful," said Helen, "army life certainly agrees with you."

"Happy Birthday Eve, darling," Derby said between hugs and kisses.

Helen Rogers had written in early July: "Derby and Eddie are as blue as indigo over your absence. I can't abide their crestfallen faces much longer. I will gladly finance a trip to Watertown for your 26th birthday, if you can arrange to spend time with us." I took Helen's letter to my company commander. He was sufficiently awed by Helen's persuasive prose to grant my request for weekend leave. He even arranged the loan of a post automobile so that I could bring my guests for a tour of the camp. The draft and large peace-time army were still sore subjects to many Americans; consequently, the military—sensitive about its image—wanted to make a good impression on the soldiers' families and friends. Helen booked rooms at the posh Woodruff Hotel. During cocktails and dinner, we all talked at once.

"I bumped into your friend Betty Hutton in the ladies room at Lord & Taylor's last week," said Derby. "She was buying a new wardrobe for her trip to Hollywood. She'd just gotten a thousand-dollar-a-week contract at Paramount Pictures. She's cute as a button and will no doubt be a big star the next time you see her."

"At 21 bucks a month, would you say I'm in the wrong business?"

"Tyler, I haven't had a decent bridge game since you went away," said Helen. While we played cards, I answered their questions about army life.

Derby, Helen and Eddie were the first civilians to visit Pine Camp since the formation of my outfit. The guys in my company were thrilled to have guests. Helen asked intelligent questions and really listened to the men's responses. She beguiled the homesick GIs lonely for maternal attention. Derby flirted with the guys and performed amusing bits of magic. Eddie regaled the soldiers with a variety of theatrical anecdotes. They asked lots of questions. "Did you ever have an unusual or embarrassing situation on stage?" Poppy inquired.

"You bet," Eddie replied. "In 1936, I did a WPA Federal Theatre tour of *The Torchbearers* in New York's five boroughs. The play satirizes Little Theatre groups. I acted the part of the effeminate stage manager. The second act opens with the cast and crew of the play-within-the-play receiving last-minute pointers from the 'grande dame' director at the final dress rehearsal. The audience views the scene as if it were backstage. I am upstage replacing bulbs in the set's footlights, bent over at the waist with my back to the audience. The old character actor tells the lady director that he has forgotten his line. Peggy Coudray—who played the director—says, 'Not to worry, Mr. Hossefosse. Everything will be all right on the night of the show. It will come. It will come.'

"One August night in Brooklyn, the playgoers howled when Peggy delivered her line, and they didn't stop. I looked back at her over my shoulder to see what was happening. She wore a terrified expression. Then in her best stage whisper she hissed, 'Edward, your balls are hanging out.' Her whisper was picked up by the microphones. The situation created havoc on both sides of both sides of the footlights. The audience went wild. Can you imagine the roar of thousands? The stage manager lowered the curtain.

"It was very hot. My shorts had gotten soppy wet during the long subway ride. I left them off when I changed into my costume. I did not know my trousers ripped when I bent over. I changed pants and the audience calmed down. After ten minutes we resumed, but as soon as Peggy said, 'It will come. It will come,' the waves of laughter made it impossible to continue. After several attempts to go on, the performance was canceled. That without doubt was my most memorable stage moment. Now my claim to fame is 'My balls were seen by thousands.'" The GIs roared almost as loud as the crowd at Prospect Park.

Fewer than half the roads on the post were paved. The sand was hot and deep. Derby struggled in her open-toed high heels. I carried her like Gary Cooper transported Marlene Dietrich across the desert in *Morocco*. Derby loved it and the men applauded and yelled. "Him, Tarzan; her, Jane!" Poppy shouted, followed by a chorus of hubba, hubbas. Eddie and Derby cheered when they saw the magazine pictures displayed in the barracks. We offered a volleyball game for the guests' entertainment followed by cake and ice cream. During the party, Eddie amused the men with a slew of bawdy jokes. "Poppy, did you hear about the hillbilly private on leave in Manhattan?" Poppy shook his head. "Well, this kid from Tennessee, who'd never been more than five miles from home before he was drafted, was strolling around mid-town. He entered Central Park and happily discovered the zoo. He liked all the animals, but he was fascinated by the big white bear. He couldn't read the description on the cage so he asked a passing attendant, 'Mister, what's that critter called?' 'That's a polar bear and he comes from the North Pole,' the worker responded. 'What's he good fer?' asked the private. 'Not much. Mainly he just eats, sleeps and sucks his paw,' explained the attendant. The private scratched his head and looked puzzled. 'Ya don't say. Well, tell me one thang; what does his Pa do?'"

That evening we cavorted at the fashionable Woodruff Nightclub. When I told Derby how beautiful she looked, she replied, "I'm always at my best in rooms lit by chandeliers." We fox-trotted the night away like typical all-American sweethearts. In our room alone, Eddie and I were so happy that I forgot to feel guilty. On Sunday morning I escorted them to the train station for a teary farewell, but we were happy because we knew I would receive leave in August. It had been a happy birthday indeed.

CHAPTER 6

Basic training ended with the 4th Armored Division engaged in a full day of drills, exams and inspections prior to all outfits passing in review for the General. The formal extravaganza was followed by athletic competitions. My team celebrated our victory with 3.2 beers in the PX. One of the men commented that if you swigged 32 bottles of the non-potent brew, you ought to get a 100 percent drunk. I loved my company. I honestly liked army life after I discovered that I could yell and bitch with the best of them. Poppy was skunking me at pool when Walter Nichols sidled up to me. "Hey, buddy. Meet me outside. We need to chew the fat."

"Sure, Walt. In five minutes at the bus stop." He was pacing when I approached him. "What's up, chum?"

"Good news, tonight!" Walt answered. "My brother is bringing my car up from Jersey this week. I found a wooded area just off the post where I can hide it. Next week when we get 36-hour passes, I plan to get my butt to Patterson to see Janet. I don't want to fart away my leave in Watertown. I figure if I get on the road by noon, I can be home by seven or eight. I already got four guys to share expenses. Do you want to come in with us?"

"You're damn straight, I do. And you can count on my buddy from Bayonne, too."

The scheme Walt devised became a weekend ritual which we inaugurated the third week in August and continued through the fall. Walt kept his '33 Chevy camouflaged with limbs in the woods where we met at noon. We uncovered Lizzie, piled in and vamoosed south. When we didn't have passes, we made arrangements with buddies to cover for us until reveille on Monday. The guys who had passes sat up, but the others became human pretzels until we were a few miles past Watertown. We took turns driving. We sang to pass the time. Walt sang, "Janet and me, and baby makes three..." Poppy sang, "Helen and me, and baby makes three..." I sang, "Just Derby and me..." When I sang the solo line, Poppy whispered, "And Eddie makes three." He'd wink and grin. A straight buddy who camped; what a hoot. I loved Poppy.

They dropped me off at the intersection of Routes 17 and 4 near the George Washington Bridge where I thumbed a ride to Manhattan. It was easy to hitch a lift in uniform. Across the river, I rode the subway to Radio City. I "quick-timed" to 52nd Street, where Eddie usually sat on the stoop anticipating my arrival. We dashed up the four flights and fell into each other's arms. Frequently, we made out in the tub. Sex while bathing was erotic and expedient since Derby expected us for dinner.

Derby and Helen habitually greeted us with loving arms and pitchers of martinis. After an hour of heavy imbibing and scintillating conversation, we dined in the hotel's renowned supper club frequented by John Barrymore when he was in New York. Occasionally we were joined by Derby's father, sister, Uncle Dwight and friends. The evenings often developed into New Year's Eve-type galas. Derby, an accomplished hostess, loved to entertain large groups.

About two a.m., Eddie and I scurried uptown to either the Dizzy Club or the Golden Pheasant. It was unusual to see soldiers in gay bars, and Eddie relished showing me off in my uniform. We always closed the bars and staggered home for one more physical session before I passed out.

At one on Sundays, we went to Derby's for brunch and bridge. She cooked in her apartment when she could plan on our exact arrival time. Edie often joined us. Sometimes we strolled and window-shopped on Fifth Avenue. At four, after a loving farewell, Eddie and I rushed back to the apartment to retrieve my knapsack, which invariably took at least two hours as I was always horny. Eddie insisted on accompanying me to meet my buddies in Jersey. All the guys knew Eddie as my civilian buddy from his visit on the post. No one questioned that he came to see me off. When we drove away, he waved vigorously and maintained a smile. What a good actor.

Only the driver stayed awake during the return trip. We changed drivers each hour. If traffic was light and the weather was favorable, we reached camp in time to cop several hours zzz's before reveille. I shuddered at the thought of being AWOL, but what the hell? Twenty-four hours in Bagdad on the Hudson was worth the risk. Fortunately, we always reached the post safely and in time for the dreaded bugle.

CHAPTER 7

"Poppy, I've been ordered to report to Colonel Baird's office immediately. We've been caught AWOL. Somebody snitched."

"I don't think so, Ty. The sergeant or C.O. handle discipline, not the commandant. Stay cool," Poppy advised, "it must be something else."

I heaved a sigh of relief when the Colonel greeted me cordially. "Corporal, I read your letter requesting a transfer to Fort Upton where you could work in government film production and radio. I believe you should be doing work for the army for which you're suited."

"Thank you, sir."

"Don't be too hasty with your thanks, Corporal. I'm denying your request."

"But, Colonel, sir..."

"The public wants to know how this peace-time army is spending their tax dollars," the Colonel interrupted. "Consequently, I've ordered the radio section of the morale branch here at Pine Camp to schedule a series of radio shows to air on WATN in Watertown over the Northern New York Network. Each battalion of the 4th Armored Division will produce a one-hour program. I want you to coordinate the Engineers segment. I decided to make it a contest. The men enjoy competitions. The best show in the series will receive a trophy, and the outfit will receive extra leave. Sunday, November 16 is your air date. You've got six weeks to create an informative and entertaining show. This is a priority assignment, and an opportunity for you to use your experience and talent for Pine Camp. I want your final script on my desk three weeks from today. Any questions?"

"No, sir. Thank you, sir. I'll get right to work on it." That afternoon I penned a short play based on an actual incident about seven raw recruits building a bridge and titled it, "What's A Pontoon?" I mailed the rough draft to Eddie and asked him to polish the dialogue and insert some gag lines.

When I arrived home on Saturday, Eddie sat on the stoop reading a script. "Here you go, kiddo," he said. "Jimmy Eanes created a masterpiece from your playlet. It's got more laugh lines than a Marx Brothers movie."

"How did you manage that?"

"The day your letter arrived, I started rehearsals for a holiday tour of *Peter Pan* with me as Captain Hook and Mr. Darling. On my way to the rehearsal hall, I met Jimmy on his way to NBC. I told him about your project. He volunteered to have a go at it. He completed it the same day, and it's perfect. You're a shoo-in to win the trophy."

That night at the Golden Pheasant, we saw Jimmy and his lover. I thanked him. "My pleasure, pal. I've always had a soft spot in my heart for men in uniform," he responded. "Actually, I just filled in some jokes I wrote for a comedy series about army life that didn't find a sponsor." He paused and I saw him mentally shift gears. "What's the scuttlebutt at your base? Are we or aren't we going to get into the war?"

"Jimmy, your guess is as good as anybody's. All signs indicate that we're revving up for all-out war."

"Jesus Christ, won't we ever learn? I lost two uncles in the last one, 'the war to end all wars.' I sure hate to think that one day you might be under fire in muddy trenches over there." He gave me a big hug. I realized that I was lucky to have friends who weren't inhibited and could express limitless support and affection.

Colonel Baird heartily endorsed my final script which included the playlet, musical selections and topical narrative. I took the announcer role. I held auditions for instrumentalists, singers and actors. I discovered a number of talented musicians, but I didn't find one experienced actor. I asked Poppy to accept a part, but he decided that weekend rehearsals and missed treks to Bayonne to see his Helen Luca were too big a sacrifice. Finally, I asked for volunteers. The seven GIs who came forth were an unpromising troupe of players, but they wanted to be "on the radio." Four of them did not read well enough to follow the script. Poppy helped me coach them until they memorized the lines. My direction was simple. "Don't try to act. Just say the words," I told them over and over. "And don't step on the laugh lines."

The day of the broadcast my company of actors suffered the identical stage fright that attacks professionals, but they came through like gangbusters. I was very proud of them. They were ecstatic. "I'm a radio star," Private Saltz proclaimed.

"Me, too. Saltz, let's be actors when we get out of the army," suggested PFC Chilimedos, a tough Armenian kid from Philadelphia. "Ty, if you keep working with me, I can be a star and put you on Easy Street."

We won the competition just as Eddie had predicted. Several weeks later with the entire 4th Armored Division present, my cast of soldiers—dressed and pomaded to perfection—and I received the trophy from Colonel Baird. The plaque was prominently displayed in the dayroom of the 24th Engineers. The men completely succumbed to the tantalizing effect that enthusiastic applause gives to "stars." They felt the magic, and briefly, the magic belonged to them.

CHAPTER 8

During the first week of December, the temperature skyrocketed to 30 under clear skies. Poppy and Walt easily convinced me to risk our ritual weekend trek on Saturday, December 6. I cabled Eddie. We made record time on my first trip south in over a month.

The draft snatched Scott Griffin in October. Eddie moved to a one-room efficiency on East 47th Street. The moment I arrived we tested the springs on his single bed for several hours before we walked to Derby's. We strolled through mid-town and enjoyed the elaborate Christmas decorations. We had a drink at the Astor Bar. We chatted about friends who had recently been drafted. "Well, seven months of your year are gone, honey boy."

"But the kicker is, you could be drafted any day," I responded. "Since Congress extended compulsory military service to 18 months for new inductees even if we don't get into the war, we could be separated for almost two years if you get called now."

"Hell, I'm 30. They won't draft old men like me." Eddie was a well of optimism. "Let's hustle. Derby won't keep the martinis cold and dry all evening. She'll drink 'em."

"Darlings, you're here at last," Derby greeted us. "Edie and I have been slaving away all afternoon preparing a 'Southern-fried' dinner to honor the return of the conquering hero of the military airwaves. Your show was splendid."

"You heard it? How?"

"Jimmy Eanes requested a transcribed recording for the files at NBC."

"It was wonderful," Edie said. "Jimmy is a fabulous writer. You boys in uniform sure know how to deliver snappy dialogue and make smooth music."

We devoured several pitchers of martinis and danced to the radio.

And while Derby's Hoppin' John did not equal my Grandma Sligh's, it was damn decent and a loving gesture. After Eddie took Edie home, I met him and Jimmy at the Golden Pheasant. I thanked Jim again for the excellent script. He toasted me, "Anything for our boys in uniform, and I do mean anything!" We hung out until the bar closed. It was our typical Saturday night.

We woke up a few minutes before one that Sunday afternoon, December 7. "Let's stay in bed the rest of the day and have sex," I suggested.

"Okay-doke, baby, but I need a cup of coffee first," Eddie rejoined.

"Mmmmm, yeah coffee. Coffee and sex, what a great combination." Eddie swatted my bare butt as he hopped out of bed. I lay there anticipating hot coffee and hot sex. I heard the water running and Eddie fiddling with the coffee pot. He turned on the radio. The music was mellow. And then, suddenly:

> We interrupt this broadcast for a special news bulletin. The Japanese have attacked Pearl Harbor, Hawaii by air, President Roosevelt has just announced. The attack was also made on all naval and military activities on the principal island of Oahu. All military leaves are canceled. Military personnel should report to their posts immediately. We repeat: the Japanese Air Force has attacked Pearl Harbor, Hawaii. Stay tuned to this station for further bulletins....

We were stunned. "Pearl Harbor! The Japanese bombed Pearl Harbor? What the hell are they talking about?" I shouted. "The Japanese ambassador is in Washington to conduct peace talks with the President. I read it in the paper yesterday."

"Maybe the situation isn't as serious as it sounds," Eddie said. "Let's try another station." He twirled the dial. Station after station echoed the identical bulletin. Finally Eddie said, "Of course, it's serious. It's damn serious. President Roosevelt announced it. It's war. Shit, piss and corruption! We're at war!" Naked and bewildered, we stood and looked at each other. We embraced. We clung. We sobbed. We went through the motions of drinking coffee, grooming and dressing in a gloomy daze.

"I must call Poppy. All leaves are canceled. I need to find out what time to be at the bridge." I rushed to the corner phone booth. At least ten people waited in line. Block after block, similar lines existed.

"Don't panic, honey boy. You can call from Derby's." Just as we reached the hotel entrance, Edie jumped out of a taxi. She ran to Eddie's open arms.

"Oh, Mr. Hossefosse. Please tell me everything will be all right on the night of the show." The three of us huddled in the middle of the sidewalk. Derby came rushing out of the lobby. The four of us hugged and kissed as our tears splashed each other like raindrops.

"Darling, I'll die if anything happens to you," Derby sobbed. "What's to become of us?"

"The Japanese started it, but we'll have to finish it. God knows, I don't want to fight with anyone, but what choice do I have?"

When I tried to call Poppy, the operator announced, "I'm sorry, sir. Long-distance calls cannot be completed at this time. All circuits are engaged due to the military emergency...."

A canopy of sadness hovered over brunch. All afternoon we listened to the radio news bulletins. "The President is meeting with members of the cabinet. Mrs. Roosevelt will speak to the nation in several hours. Stay tuned to this station for further updates...." So much news. So little information. After a blubbery farewell with Derby and her family, Eddie and I headed uptown for perhaps our final magic hours.

On the streets, thousands dashed helter-skelter to get where they thought they needed to be, but many hesitated long enough to acknowledge my uniform. Some waved. Some saluted. Others spoke. "Hi, soldier." "Good luck, Corporal." "Be brave, son." Suddenly strangers connected. Everyone realized that we were in the midst of an historical event of enormous proportions.

Eddie and I spent an hour on his single bed just being close. Our desire for sex was thwarted by the fear of constant separation. We envisioned a bleak future.

Eddie went with me to Jersey. It was the same trip we had made numerous times, but it was different. For all we knew, I might ship out to Hawaii the next day. We held hands as we walked up the ramp in the dark. We tried to say positive things, but words failed. The only thing we were certain about was our mutual love.

Walt's old Chevy was parked at the intersection. After handshakes with Eddie, we piled in and headed north. I watched Eddie out the back window. He waved until we were out of sight.

CHAPTER 9

President Roosevelt convened Congress on Monday, December 8. He requested and received a declaration of war on Japan. That night, when the President addressed the nation, every man at Pine Camp was part of the radio audience of 90 million who heard him state, "We are going to win the war and...the peace that follows." We believed him. On Thursday, Germany and Italy declared war on the United States; we reciprocated. By the end of the week, war stretched around the world.

GIs' attitudes changed. We forgot that we were promised release at the end of one year. Being a soldier became serious business. We believed in our cause. Bus loads of new recruits and gung-ho volunteers arrived on the post hourly. By the end of 1942, Pine Camp would be the second largest training camp in the nation. We went on maneuvers to test men, equipment and weapons. Twice our company went on attack at midnight in blackout across a 200-mile stretch of rugged terrain in 30-below temperatures. I acted as platoon sergeant from the turret of one of the leading tanks. Before we could hit the sack after 48 sleepless hours, we had to clean and organize our weapons and gear for regular duty. The accelerated pace was horrendous.

Santa Claus arrived for me the week before Christmas. Major James Mason, officer designated to develop a morale service unit, summoned me to post headquarters. Sergeant Lane, the Major's secretary, had performed a sensational piano solo on the Engineers radio program. When the Major expressed his need for an enlisted man with theatrical experience, Sergeant Lane recommended me. I discovered that breaks in the military, like breaks in show business, are often a combination of who you know and being in the right place. At the interview, Sergeant Lane reiterated his admiration for my direction of the radio show. Major Mason asked me to give a summary of my professional background, and he listened attentively while I enumerated my credits.

"Corporal, now that we are at war, each branch of the military will swell to mammoth numbers. The War Department knows that entertainment and recreation on each post are essential to morale. What I need is an enlisted man to take charge of a unit to provide live entertainment utilizing the talents of the men on the post. Can you do that?"

"Yes, sir. Yes, sir, I can," I eagerly replied. "I can organize a theatre workshop to give plays and revues the men will love."

"Theatre workshop, eh? I like the sound of that. What will you need?"

"A place to work. A space large enough to build scenery and rehearse. A musical director and a good piano. And a technical director with unlimited access to tools, sir."

"Corporal, you're my man. I'll requisition what you need in my name. Give Sergeant Lane your list, and we'll avoid a lot of red tape."

Back in the barracks, Poppy greeted me with the official word, "No holiday leave for anyone. Damn, we're stranded in this freaking ice palace, and it's cold enough to freeze the nuts off a Jeep."

"*Petticoat Fever*, that's the ticket," I responded.

"Huh?" Poppy sported a puzzled expression.

"*Petticoat Fever*, it's the perfect choice for our first production." Then I backed up and told him about my interview with the Major. "Poppy, you know electricity, and you know construction and tools. I want you to be the technical director."

"Sure, buddy, whatever you say. Now tell me about *Petticoat Fever*."

"It's a three-act comedy that parallels our situation. A wireless radio operator is snowbound in 40-below temperatures in Labrador. He has not seen a woman in two years when two beautiful young ladies enter his celibate existence. It's perfect. The men will immediately identify with the hero's plight and the setting. It's a laugh riot."

"That sounds great. We sure need some laughs around here."

I asked Sergeant Lane to be the musical director, but he declined and recommended his friend, Private Angelo La Mariana who had a degree in music. Angelo was excited as Poppy to accept the challenge. On Christmas Eve I reported my progress to Major Mason. The Major issued requests to transfer Angelo and Poppy, which Colonel Selten promptly honored.

When the officer in charge of the 24th Engineers Battalion, nicknamed Major Bottleass, discovered that the Colonel had approved the transfers, Bottleass blew his stack. He avowed that he had great plans for LaPolla as a draftsman and officer, but it was too late to reverse the action. It was my second conflict with Major Bottleass. He busted me when I did not accept assignment to OCS, but Major Mason reinstated me two days later when I transferred to post headquarters. Twice I outmaneuvered Bottleass. My private war with the army had commenced, and I won the early battles.

As I planned each phase of the workshop, I consulted Eddie by letter. On December 19, the U.S. Office of Censorship began operation. All incoming and outgoing mail was read by security inspectors. I casually joked in a letter that I didn't want my plans for the workshop bandied about since I feared another entertainment unit might steal my thunder. Eddie wisely interpreted that I requested him to avoid anything in his letters that might prove embarrassing. He used feminine names when he mentioned gay friends. His letters were campier than ever, and we considered it good sport to fool the censors.

Even though we were denied Yule leave, we had a decent holiday. We made ornaments and decorated the barracks. The army provided several traditional Christmas dinners. Most of the guys shared their gifts and letters with buddies. Mother sent a box of homemade candied grapefruit peel which provided Poppy and the others a new taste treat. Derby sent several pounds of fudge. Auntie Estelle and Grandma sent fruitcakes. Eddie sent the *Petticoat Fever* scripts which Poppy, Angelo and I avidly read, and we began making plans. Eddie's play, *Peter Pan*, received a good review in *The New York Times* on New Year's Eve. Even though I yearned to be with Eddie and Derby for the holidays, I was totally optimistic about my future as a soldier. I was going to do the work I loved for the army. Only one major glitch loomed on my horizon. *Petticoat Fever* required two pretty comediennes and there was not one female stationed at Pine Camp.

CHAPTER 10

Major Mason obtained a self-contained building with ample room to meet all needs plus living quarters. Angelo, Poppy and I moved in on New Year's Eve. We cleaned, repaired and painted, in addition to our regular duties training new recruits. Thoughts of *Petticoat Fever* dominated every minute of my 18-hour work day. The Major kindly excused us from standing reveille. I began auditions for the six male roles. A small number came forward, but not one of them possessed the experience to essay the leading role. If our first production flopped, my tenure as director of the Pine Camp Theatre Workshop might be short-lived. "Stop worrying, Ty. You play the lead," Poppy suggested.

"That's easier said than done. How would I direct the other actors? The lead is onstage throughout the entire play. If I do the part, I will need a co-director to sit out front to see that my direction is falling into place." Poppy sported a sly grin. Then he sang his infamous solo line. Poppy was right. Who better than Eddie? "And Derby and Edie can play the femme leads," I responded.

"Why not? Everybody's volunteering for war work." When Poppy said it, it sounded so logical, but I had visions of Major Mason having a stroke when I proposed something so unorthodox. I told Poppy that before I suggested it to the Major, I really ought to consult my three friends.

Several days later when the Major came to view the building renovations, he told me that Colonel Selten had received orders for us to attend a five-day planning conference on the army's new morale division, Special Service Companies, for overseas duty. "The army is going into show business in a big way," the Major said. "Special Services will provide programs of recreation, entertainment and information for all branches of the American Armed Forces and our allies around the world."

Colonel Selten, Major Mason and I traveled to New York by train. I received permission to stay with Eddie rather than be billeted with them. The conference was held at army headquarters on Governors Island. All-day planning sessions were conducted by representatives from the War Department, USO leaders and civilian members of the entertainment industry including Antoinette Perry, president of the American Theatre Wing, plus Louis Simon and Edward Hale from Actors Equity. The range of activities planned for Special Services was unparalleled in military history. The design called for the creation of 41 outfits each made up of 109 combat-trained men and five officers separated into four platoons. Each platoon would be built around a core of specialists from each of six specialty sections:

(1) Education Section – libraries, lectures, news bulletins, religious services and publications
(2) Athletic Section – games, equipment, instruction and repairs
(3) Cinema Section – feature Hollywood films, training films, film and projector repair and circulation
(4) Radio Section – public address systems, announcements, recorded music, transcriptions and equipment repairs
(5) Music Section – dance bands, concert groups, instruments and repairs, Army Hit Kit of Popular Songs and performances
(6) Theatre Section – variety shows, skits, make-up, costumes and technical assistance for USO touring shows

Each conference participant left Governors Island each day with his creative juices flowing. I felt honored to be a part of this august group making important decisions, but my greatest thrill was the opportunity to convince Eddie, Edie and Derby to participate in *Petticoat Fever*. Eddie said yes without hesitating. Edie declined due to family responsibilities. "Derby, honey, I want you for my leading lady in *Petticoat Fever*."

"Do I have to join the army?"

"No, but you'll have to live on the post and eat army chow for a month."

"I may appear to you as a spoiled, little rich girl, but whatever is good enough for the American GI is good enough for me. I'd eat bread and water to star in a major production." When I told her that Edie was unavailable, Derby said, "I know just the actress for you, Minelda Lange. She's anxious to do war work. She's a dynamic, seasoned performer with Broadway credits and everything. I'll invite her to dinner."

"Great. Invite Major Mason and Colonel Selten. You and Minelda can display your charms so that when I make my proposal to request you, they can't refuse." Minelda was pretty, witty and elegant. The two of them beguiled the brass at Derby's grand soiree. The Colonel and the Major had a swell time hobnobbing with Eddie and Derby's family and friends.

Every night Eddie and I went to our favorite hangouts. Suddenly, it was not unusual to see soldiers, sailors and marines in gay bars. Since Pearl Harbor, every place in New York was crowded with men in uniform.

During the return train trip, Colonel Selten said, "We need to get a production mounted as soon as possible if we're going to keep up with the other posts in the Second Corps Area."

The next day I presented my proposal to Major Mason. I started off with big items such as requisitioning Derby, Minelda and Eddie. I supplied details about their living arrangements and transportation. Then I moved on to rehearsal schedules, building materials and budget. I concluded by requesting the use of a command car and driver two nights a week to transport the two young women from the Watertown Little Theatre who had agreed to play the small roles of Eskimo women. During my presentation, Major Mason stared at me as if I were speaking a foreign language. Finally, he spoke. "Good God, Carpenter. Do you think I can do the impossible? There's a war on, and you're proposing things that have never been done before." We shared a long silence. "Can't you use soldiers to play the girls' parts?"

"No, sir. Never," I insisted. "We have two classy, professional actresses who are donating their talents to the war effort. With them, our show will be first rate. It has to be my way if we're going to do the show that Colonel Selten wants. Believe me, sir, I know what I'm doing."

"I pray to God you do because I sure as hell don't." After a pregnant pause he said, "All right, son. But if you fail, it's your ass."

"Yes, sir. It will be my ass. I'm not afraid."

"Well, if you're that sure, then I'm sure too. Tell me again what you need, and I'll try to work it out."

CHAPTER 11

A week later Derby, Minelda and Eddie were comfortably ensconsed on the post and at work preparing for our opening on February 26, 1942. Sergeant Phil Johnson, who entered the service straight from managing *Hellzapoppin!* on Broadway, designed the set and supervised construction. Poppy did the technical work and proved to be a wise choice. Each day while I put new recruits through basic, Eddie accomplished the 1001 things required to ensure smooth rehearsals. He borrowed Bob Haig's formal attire. Bob wrote that he was happy to donate "my tail, I mean tails" to the war effort. Eddie repeatedly called Private Andrew E. Dennis, Jr. by his character's name, Kimo, and created another lifelong nickname. Other members of the cast were PFC Christopher Williams, PFC Stephen Bahorski, Private Gene Straub, Private Martin Preville, Althea Green and Helen Chapin. Angelo assembled a 25-piece orchestra to play his original overture which incorporated patriotic themes and popular melodies such as "I've Got My Love to Keep Me Warm," and "I Don't Want to Set the World on Fire."

Major Mason gave us free rein as he was totally preoccupied with getting other sections of the 1209th Service Unit established. During the final week of rehearsals, Actors Equity sent officer Lou Simon to assist us. His polishing touches boosted our morale. Our final dress rehearsal was a mess. Derby was very nervous, and her timing was off. All of us were guilty of trying too hard, and that compounded her insecurity.

On opening night the thermometer registered 20 degrees below. The 3000-seat War Department Theatre—three times the size of the average Broadway house—was packed. While we waited in the wings, Kimo tapped Derby on the shoulder. "Knock, knock," he whispered.

"Who's there?"

"Felix."

"Felix who?"

"Feel excited?" When Derby laughed and flashed her best ingenue smile, we saw her relax. Kimo's thoughtful action was just the right touch to ease everyone's tension. The audience responded with thunderous applause for the overture. Five minutes into the play, I knew from their reactions that the sex-starved GIs with nothing but "Lady Five Fingers" to relieve their frozen balls identified with the hero's situation. When Derby entered wearing a clinging, bright red sweater, she knocked the men's socks off. They whistled, screamed and stomped for a full five minutes. A half-dozen curtain calls to deafening applause confirmed that we had done our work well. General Gillespie ordered Major Mason to take a bow. The band played, and the cast, joined by the audience, sang a rousing finale of popular songs.

Sergeant Ed Cooke, editor of the post paper, wrote a glowing review. In it he included an interview with a soldier. "'Did you enjoy *Petticoat Fever?*'" The private replied, "'I sure did. Them actresses from New York City were prettier than movie stars, and the fellow who played the main part was almost as funny as Cary Grant in *Bringing Up Baby.*'" That young GI's reaction was the review we wanted.

The next morning Major Mason summoned Eddie to his office. When Eddie returned, he was grinning form ear to ear. The Major had suggested that Eddie enlist as soon as possible and not wait to be drafted. The Major would request him to be assigned to the 1209th. Eddie did a marvelous imitation of the Major when he reported the details of their conversations. "By God, Fuller, we know what you can do. I'm not going to let another outfit cash in on a talent we need." Poppy and I whooped like Geronimo and danced around the pot-bellied stove. When I drove Eddie to the train in Watertown, we sang and laughed. We were the gayest gay men in the world. I knew that with Eddie beside me, I could face whatever the war might bring.

The demand for tickets doubled our run. Minutes before our final performance, Major Mason met with us. He explained in a serio-comedic manner that the War Department had ordered us to begin a tour at West Point on March 29, with 18 posts before we closed on April 19. The Major said that we were an important part of the largest soldier-theatre project in the history of the U.S. Army. Five productions with 91 soldier actors and technicians would travel 8,000 miles and play to an estimated audience of 200,000. Too good to be true, the ax fell the next day. I had the arduous task of telling the cast that the four GIs from the 4th Armored Division must be replaced by men assigned to the 1209th. Derby and Minelda rushed back to New York so that they could return in ten days to rehearse with the new cast.

Fortunately, a number of professional actors had been assigned to me for basic training, and I chose replacements who were at least as good as the originals and considerably more experienced. Private Chet Cooper, a Carnegie Tech graduate with four Broadway credits, joined the cast, as did Privates Walter Bombard and Gerald Van Hee. Sergeant Phil Johnson took over from Poppy as technical director and stage manager. Poppy served as his assistant and made his acting debut as a sailor. We traveled in two weapons carriers and used a six-by-six to transport the switchboard, sets, props and costumes. At each post the army supplied two females to play the non-speaking Eskimo women and six GIs who helped us unload, set up, strike the set and reload.

On April 1, we arrived at Camp Upton for a two-day run. Eddie was sent to Upton as his marshaling area to await assignment. I rushed to headquarters. When I asked the company clerk where I could find Eddie, he told me that Eddie shipped out that morning with 300 other new recruits. "Where?" I asked.

The clerk sifted through mounds of paper on his desk. "I think it was an Infantry Division in Mississippi." Total panic enveloped me.

"Are you sure?" I pleaded. "He was supposed to be sent to Pine Camp."

"Sorry, buddy. I can't find the list, but I'm sure he's on the train to Biloxi. He's probably somewhere in West Virginia by this time." I stumbled out to the street and let the tears flow. I lost my bearing and couldn't find my way back to the theatre. My soul ached. Then, I heard Derby calling my name. I turned and saw a giggling Derby racing down a side street with Eddie in tow. He wore fatigues. Now, he was a soldier, too! I exploded with joy. I grabbed Eddie's hand and showered Derby with the hugs and kisses I wanted to lavish on Eddie.

Eddie happily explained, "After reveille, I was told to report to the Rec Hall for all-day detail. I'm one of your six stagehands. Now, ain't that a hoot?" If I had gone into the Rec Hall with the rest of the company, I could have avoided a lot of pain. The army had taught me to be assertive, but that day my assertiveness created the cruelest April Fool's joke ever played on me. We left Eddie at Upton and proceeded to Fort Totten where we learned that our tour had been extended for two additional weeks at three more army camps, plus Yale and Princeton.

Minelda's agent was pulling his hair out as he had her lined up for a radio series, and Derby needed to return to school so that she could graduate with her class; however, those were minor issues easily resolved since businesses and institutions were flexible and accommodating toward individuals engaged in war work.

On March 30, we had played at Fort Jay on Governors Island. *The New York Daily News* ran a picture of Derby and a feature about the production. Derby's family, many classmates and teachers attended a performance as did Edie, Bob Haig and Jimmy Eanes. When we played Fort Dix, Poppy parents and Helen Luca saw the show. Poppy's parents were so proud. Helen went bananas when she saw how handsome he looked in his sailor costume. At Yale, Minelda's parents and my cousin Linda Ceresole and family were in the audience. On Friday, April 10, popular *Daily Mirror* columnist Nick Kenny concluded his jubilant review of us by stating, "Miss Rogers is definitely headed for Broadway." We ended the tour with three encore performances at Pine Camp. We had performed Mark Reed's non-topical farce 69 times in six weeks; the equivalent of a two-month run on Broadway.

CHAPTER 12

Eddie leaped into army life with the grace of a dancer. He wanted to be a good soldier and worked at it. I taught him everything I knew during basic training. I was very proud of him. We joked that we were the standard-bearers of ancient Greek tradition. Poppy offered to teach Eddie to drive, but Eddie balked. As a teenager, he had wrecked his father's car, and he never drove again.

While we were on tour, the 1209th had quadrupled. According to the 1940 census there were 6,931 working actors in the country and by mid-1942, 3,503 of them were in the military. The man who made his living as an actor was among the most expendable in civilian life, but considered essential to the war effort. The proportion of actors drafted far exceeded all other professions except musicians, who ran a close second. Now, we had some recognizable names among our ranks: Stuart Churchill from Fred Waring's band; Johnny Ryan from Ben Bernie's orchestra; Dudley Gilbert, the funny half of a nightclub act with straight man/singer Robert Alda; opera singers Steven Kennedy and Lloyd Harris; concert violinist and Broadway singer/dancer Sammy Becker; ballet dancer Leonard Kane; scenic/lighting designer Clay Yurdin, who had three shows on Broadway when he was drafted; and conductor Harold Hanwacker (a.k.a. Hal Hastings). Major Louis W. Bleser joined the 1209th. Every man in the company loved and respected Major Bleser for his musical talents and compassionate leadership. Our shared admiration for him helped us to respect each other and united the company.

We weren't exclusively producing shows and living in the fast lane in 1942. That was the fun part of army life. During the first half of the year, the war news was devastating. The Japanese were blitzing our navy in the Pacific, and the Nazis were thrashing the Allied Forces in North Africa and Russia. Our naval victory at Midway Island in June gave us hope and made us more determined. Major Bleser increased the already rigorous requirements of basic for the entertainers. He wanted us to be the best combat-trained infantrymen in the army so that we could protect ourselves and others when the time came. And we all knew that the time would come when we would be shipped overseas to fight.

After Angelo went to OCS, Eddie and Phil Johnson moved into the workshop with Poppy and me. Poppy occasionally kept Phil occupied elsewhere so that Eddie and I could have some private time. Poppy was aces in all departments.

Eddie and I developed a variety entertainment, *Let's Have Fun!*, which played at the Service Club on Wednesdays and Fridays to packed houses. Each week we presented a completely new show consisting of a one-act play, a vocalist and trio, a standup comic and a male stripper who camped more than stripped. It was my first experience with drag acts. The irony of our drag shows was that none of our "strippers" were gay; they were heterosexual men who loved to entertain. We also added post hospital shows to our roster of activities.

Phil Johnson supervised the renovation of the Post Rec Hall for our exclusive use. Eddie decided to stage *Squaring the Circle*, a comedy about Communist Russia, in our new theatre as a patriotic gesture and dedicated the performance to our Russian allies. Eddie had appeared in both the Broadway production and the national tour. Seven soldiers, Eddie and I, and two local girls—Rosemary Byer and Jacqueline Keenan—romped on stage for 16 performances before packed houses of laughing GIs.

In late June I received a ten-day furlough and went to visit my family in Jacksonville. My brother Edward had just graduated high school and joined the navy. William and Buddy were chomping at the bit to leave school and join the service, too, but Mother and I convinced them to wait until they graduated. Even 14-year-old Pat wanted to get into service. I worked out at the YMCA where I met a lieutenant, a private and a staff sergeant who were in the closet, but, when you know who you are, the closet gets bigger. It was wonderful to meet other gay men in uniform, but it was a secret that I could tell no one except another gay. I didn't feel guilty about being physical with other servicemen. I felt perfectly secure in my love for Eddie. Sexual jealousy did not play a part in our life together. It would be easy to blame or excuse this attitude on the war; many people did. We were simply sexually liberated individuals. After I accepted my homosexuality, I worked at protecting myself and other gays from bigoted abuse. I regretted that my family and army colleagues were totally incapable of accepting the real me.

While I was home on leave, Poppy took and passed the written and physical exams for the Army Air Corps. Only men who scored in the superior range on the Stanford-Binet Intelligence Test were accepted for flight training. The Air Corps was so eager to get Poppy that he transferred out in 48 hours. "Poppy wouldn't have left if you had been here," Eddie moaned.

"Yes, he would have," I replied. "All his life he's dreamed of being a pilot. I'm happy for him, but I will miss my true-blue buddy. Poppy's like President Roosevelt—an intellectual giant with an immeasurable heart and soul. If only he'd been gay, he would be perfect."

"The world needs good straight men, too," Eddie mused. "I hope Poppy has at least 100 kids, all like him."

Civic organizations in Watertown and Carthage constantly requested performers from the 1209th, and Major Bleser attempted to honor all requests. We did a number of benefits for the Red Cross, and we were especially excited when the Army and Navy Post #61 of the American Legion wanted to sponsor a big show to benefit the Army Emergency Relief Fund.

CHAPTER 13

After the *Petticoat Fever* tour, Derby began her second phase of war work. The student body of the American Academy of Dramatic Arts volunteered to serve at the Stage Door Canteen for the duration. The Canteen, operated by the American Theatre Wing, opened on March 2, 1942 across from Shubert Alley on West 44th Street. As a Junior Hostess three nights a week, Derby's duties were to dance with the servicemen and KP (kitchen police), two of her favorite activities. She graduated with honors in June and immediately landed a job in a summer tour of *Mr. and Mrs. North*, featuring film star Nancy Carroll. Edie Groome became Mrs. Sergeant Porter Leach on a hot, Saturday, July afternoon at the "Little Church Around the Corner." She wrote Eddie that she would love him forever, and it was her heart's desire that he and Porter, a handsome marine, be friends. Edie's advancement in advertising was so pronounced that she dropped all aspirations for a theatrical career.

Irving Berlin's all-soldier show, *This Is The Army*, opened in New York on July 4th to rave reviews. Every song became an instant hit. The noted composer auditioned hundreds of entertainers from army installations all over the country, including most of the performers at Pine Camp. After thoughtful deliberation, Eddie and I elected not to audition since it might mean separation. We were content to stay together doing work we loved. From our post, Mr. Berlin chose Stuart Churchill and gave him a prominent solo, "I'm Getting Tired So I Can Sleep." The profits from *This Is The Army* were Mr. Berlin's contribution to the Army Emergency Relief Fund, which assisted the families of soldiers who needed financial aid to pay for such items as coal, fuel oil, doctors' bills, funeral expenses and even layettes.

When the American Legion requested to sponsor a Pine Camp show for the AERF, we devoted hours to creating a revue to showcase all the men's talents, but we felt pressured to be original and not produce a poor-man's version of *This Is The Army*. The other blockbuster on Broadway was Mike Todd's burlesque extravaganza *Star and Garter*, starring Gypsy Rose Lee. Eddie suggested a satire of that smash called *Stars Without Garters*, indicating an all-male burlesque.

Phil went on leave to Manhattan to see *Star and Garter* and Gae Foster. Phil broke into show business as a dancer with the Gae Foster Belles and Beaux at the Roxy. Gae had also given me my big break when she hired me for the *Aquacade* at the World's Fair. When Phil told Gae about our pending production, she made many suggestions for imaginative staging and donated hundreds of costumes from the Roxy collection. With a profusion of female attire worth thousands, we decided to cast fifteen local girls and have our title refer to the rubber shortage. All across the nation, women donated their garters and girdles to scrap rubber drives. Eddie wrote music and lyrics for the opening: "We're stars without garters, elastic no more. We're stars without garters, we're just rubber poor!"

Eddie's mother visited Pine Camp for three days in August. Eddie introduced me as his best and dearest friend, the one he had been writing about for the past year and a half. Mrs. Fuller enjoyed sitting in on rehearsals and meeting all the guys. At the time, Ronald, Eddie's brother, was en route with his infantry troop to the South Pacific.

We held rehearsals in several locations. Phil drilled the girls at the USO in Watertown. I rehearsed the skits at the workshop while Sasha London practiced the singers and band in the Rec Hall. By Labor Day, we put all the parts together and began previews for the men on the post. In deference to gas rationing, we transported the girls from town by army truck. We juggled and revised until we had 25 outstanding segments. Phil's inventive choreography—naughty-but-nice bumps and grinds—combined with elegant costumes, helped the 15 girls achieve a degree of professionalism beyond our expectations. Twenty soldiers had star turns in four skits, blackouts or musical solos. The total cast acted as chorus accompanied by a 20-piece orchestra. The original music and lyrics created by Eddie and Chet Cooper—"We are the Pine Camp nuts; no ifs, no ands, no butts"—and topical jokes—"First Soldier: 'Did you hear about the WAAF who backed into an airplane propeller?' Second Soldier: 'No, what happened?' First Soldier: 'Dis-assed-er.'"—provided tasteful amusement as pure as the driven Nancy Drew! The premier of Major Bleser's march, "Semper Vigilantes," with the cast in military parade dress brought the house down. We played at the Avon Theatre the week of September 26 and raised thousands of dollars for the AERF. *Stars Without Garters* was the lead item in theatre critic Burns Mantle's October 1 column in *The New York Daily News*. What a thrill to be declared an unqualified hit by the dean of critics!

CHAPTER 14

"We're going to put Pine Camp on the map with a coast-to-coast, hour-long, live CBS radio broadcast on Tuesday, October 20 at 9:30 p.m.," Private Kermit Schafer, the company publicity director, announced to the 100-plus men of the 1209th seated in the Rec Hall. "Our segment of the radio program, 'Cheers From The Camps,' will do for us what *This Is The Army* did for Fort Upton. Ty, in his capacity of producer/director, will be in charge."

We were excited. Except for the hospital shows and *Let's Have Fun!* at the service club, we postponed other activities until after the big broadcast; however, Eddie and Phil weren't content without a major stage production in the works. They planned our next show, an old-fashioned melodrama with Gay Nineties songs. They insisted that Derby play the heroine. God love Major Mason. He issued passes for Eddie and me to have a New York weekend of business and revelry. Derby jumped at the chance for another star turn at Pine Camp. Our frolic in the Big Apple was short due to transportation difficulties. The combination of gas rationing and military mobility had created an unusual demand on railroads, so we took what was available and decided to spend the extra night at the Woodruff Hotel. We were seated three to a seat, instead of two facing three on the opposite seat. A tall, handsome young civilian faced me. We chatted, and by the time we completed the seven-hour trek with our long legs intertwined, we were fast friends. Robert Cadigan—a brakeman from Long Island transferred due to railway expansion created by military demands—showed us a snapshot of his wife and children. I showed him a picture of Derby and told him about our mission to Manhattan. He and Eddie got along like a house afire, what with Eddie's vast knowledge of trains learned from his father's occupation. When we arrived in Watertown, Eddie invited Robert for drinks at the Woodruff Tap Room. We drank until the bar closed, and

Robert joined us in our room.

The three of us—naked in that big, double bed—explored each other in ways I couldn't have imagined when we met on the train. The next morning, Robert walked us to the bus station, where we exchanged courteous farewells and promises to keep in touch. "Eddie, I just passed two major milestones. I had sex with a married man, and I experienced a menage à trois."

Eddie chuckled and slapped me on the back. "Well, baby, I bet it won't be your last time for either."

When we returned to the post, Guy Della Chioppa, the CBS director, and John Lund, the writer, had just arrived. We met with them and discussed the format and types of talent available. For contrast, John chose to divide the host duties between a soldier and Ted Husing, CBS newsman. I nominated Eddie for that spot. A soldier's letter to his family detailing his use of military equipment in sub-zero temperatures as preparation for victory in Europe was the unifying feature. I delivered the radio letter which was divided into quarter segments and combined with appropriate dramatic skits and musical selections. Ever mindful of our "good neighbor policy," the band offered a rousing rendition of "Mexican Hat Dance," and Corporal Earle Weidman sang Brazil's popular folk song, "Ma Ma Yo Quiero." "Go Down Moses" sung by Private Lloyd Harris and a choral rendition of "Onward Christian Soldiers" provided religious significance. "Caissons Go Rolling Along," "Praise The Lord And Pass The Ammunition" and Major Bleser's march added the right military touch. For the hepcats, Private Arthur Engler sang "It Ain't What You Do" and Sergeant Paul Dolbey played a xylophone solo, "Frolic On The Keys." Private Elliot Magaziner performed a masterful violin rendition of "Rondo Capriccioso" for the long-haired listener. Private Johnny Ryan sang the pop hit "I Came Here To Talk For Joe" to satisfy the bobbysoxers' need for a love song. CBS musical director Harry Salter rehearsed the vocalists, instrumentalists and two bands for three days.

Eddie wrote a verse narrative which he delivered between choruses of "Hills Of Home" sung by Private Steven Kennedy:

> The trail leads always to the east toward the rising sun.
> Our campfires dot the trail behind and the task must still be done.
> Whether under blazing heat or in the chill of night,
> Our labor is for freedom's cause. We keep that goal in sight!
> But there are times when still we lie beneath a blue and silent sky,

Or watch the flames leap up and glow when forest shadows shrink and
Grow. Then our thoughts turn back along the way and once again
We see a face and hear a song, a few notes stray. And for a time
It seems the day when soldiers all, we cease to roam
And march the winding road to home.

Dudley Gilbert delivered a comic monologue, and we did a skit about Chaplain William Macquire at Pearl Harbor as a tribute to the navy. At the closing, Sergeant Andrew "Kimo" Dennis sent greetings to his family in Idaho, and Private Mario Machado, a naturalized citizen, addressed his fiancee in Recife, Brazil.

Ted Husing arrived at seven and we began a chaotic rehearsal; but, we accomplished what CBS wanted. Not one mistake occurred on the broadcast, and our 3,000 cheering soldier-audience let the nation know that morale was high at Pine Camp. The show was unabashedly sentimental, but the war years were a sentimental era. Civilians and soldiers had faith in each other, and we were proud to announce our faith in our government and our leaders.

"Cheers From The Camps" put Pine Camp on the map as Kermit had predicted. Fan mail arrived the next day and continued to come in for weeks. Many letters were from people who had relatives in the military, or people we hadn't heard from in years. Each letter expressed thanks for our sacrifices and stated that we were included in their prayers. Artie Engler received a telegram: "Job open in Norfolk, Virginia nightclub. $55 a week. Wire when available." Scat singer Artie return-wired, "Available right after the war. Uncle Sam holds option on me for the duration." Eminent composer Aaron Copland sent Steven Kennedy a congratulatory wire. A girl in Texas sent several songs for future broadcasts, and a solicitous lady from Missouri inquired whether the boys at Pine Camp had sufficient flannel underwear to last throughout the cold winter ahead. Mr. W.M. Smith—father of my Tallahassee high-school girlfriend Emma Laurie—wrote, "After you and the other American soldiers have whipped those anti-Christ Germans and those skunk-like Japsnakes, you should get a good job on the radio...." Eddie's hometown paper carried a review of the show which ended, "Newburg is proud of this fine young man who was reared and educated here." Eddie's parents sent a huge box of chocolates, which most agreed was the ultimate fan letter.

CHAPTER 15

In 1939 Eddie had appeared on Broadway opposite Jacqueline Susann in an adaptation of an old-fashioned melodrama, *Little Lost Sister*, with a spiffy new title, *She Gave Them All She Had*. Eddie wrote the 90-year-old author, A.J. Pegler, to obtain a copy of the original. Mr. Pegler sent a script and production notes for the 1898 premiere. He wrote that he would include us in his prayers that the war would soon end. We decided to recreate the 1898 version, but keep the 1939 title. Derby arrived on November 1 amid a fanfare of publicity in the New York, Syracuse and Watertown papers. Eddie cast local girls, Nina Riche and Belle Scott, as the mother and sister plus himself as the hero, Ray Fairthorne as the model boy, Kimo Dennis as the financier, Dudley Gilbert as the old sot, and me as the villain. I contacted Brooks Costumes in New York to rent wardrobe for the principal players. To our delight, Brooks donated everything we needed.

For the olios—between-the-acts musical numbers and skits—we engaged 13 area girls to portray Gay Nineties' belles. For their partners, I cast every available man who could carry a tune and move his feet at the same time. The cast totaled 35, plus 15 musicians directed by Eliot Magaziner. Phil dressed the chorus in dozens of eye-catching costumes from the Gae Foster donation. Phil supervised the construction of a runway from the stage into the audience area, which he refurbished with tables and chairs. One evening during rehearsals Phil commented, "Have you noticed that most of the characters in the comics are doing war work? Daddy Warbucks, Popeye, Superman, I guess Mutt and Jeff will be next."

"They already are. They changed their names to Willie and Joe and joined the infantry," Eddie quipped. That exchange led to Ray Fairthorne and Santo Commando painting caricatures in vivid colors like the funnies on the blackout windows. Checkered tablecloths and hurricane candle lamps added to the Music Hall ambiance. The cast and crew doubled as waiters who served ten-cent beers and free pretzels.

On November 7, when 400,000 USA-British Forces commanded by General Eisenhower landed in North Africa, we shouted with joy. It helped offset the horrendous news reported that same week by Allied authorities in London, who confirmed that since the war began in 1939, the Nazis had killed at least 500,000 Europeans and had shipped thousands—perhaps millions—of Polish, French and German Jews, Gypsies, Jehovah's Witnesses and homosexuals to concentration camps.

President Roosevelt's Thanksgiving Proclamation on November 11 revived our national pride when he reported that the Allies' greatest asset was the industrial strength of the United States. In 1942, in an effort called the "Miracle of Production," the USA churned out enough supplies for its troops and the besieged populations of Britain, China, Russia and other countries fighting invaders. Bing-bam-boff-zowie! Reason enough to sling the slang.

During rehearsals Derby exhibited uncharacteristic behavior. She screamed like a banshee and acted the perfect bitch about one of her costumes. "It makes me look like an over-ripe soufflé!" she yelled at Phil. I agreed about the dress but reminded her that Phil was the designer. She accepted my reaction, but she wasn't happy. A few days later, we were in the workshop going over lines. She suddenly dropped character and said, "Well, I guess Minelda was right."

"What are you talking about, Derby?"

"While we were on tour with *Petticoat Fever*, many times Minelda advised me that our relationship would end in nothing. She said I was a fool to ignore all the good-looking guys on your account because you are so much in love with Eddie that you don't have room in your life for me. Was she right?"

"Dear God," I thought, "what do I say?"

At that dramatic moment, Kimo burst through the door. He explained that he had misplaced his tap shoes. After he finally found them, the three of us rushed to the mess hall. At last I understood Derby's enigmatic behavior. I did not tell Eddie about the confrontation; it was my problem.

The subject of our relationship did not come up again. Derby had spoken and obviously that temporarily satisfied her. At dress rehearsal Derby wore a vastly altered version of the dress Phil assigned her. She looked stunning. She had used her sewing talent and sense of style for the good of the show. Phil broke the ice and expressed what all of us felt. "Hubba, Hubba. Derby, you look sensational."

On Thanksgiving—November 26 and the day before our opening—CBS repeated our "Cheers From The Camps" segment as a holiday special. Ted Husing announced that the 1209th won the prize for best show in the series. It was great fun to listen to ourselves on national radio. Afterwards we went to the Service Club for beers and dancing. Derby said it was the most atmospheric Thanksgiving ever.

The post newspaper in a rave review of *She Gave Them All She Had* dubbed Derby "Pine Camp's Own Star and Favorite Pinup." The men howled at the drag acts: Dudley and Lloyd doing "Daisy, Daisy" and Sammy Becker as the lead cancan dancer backed by six high-kicking girls. The GIs loved sipping a foamy beverage while watching Helen James as Little Nell and Dudley as the dirty villain sing, "I'm In Love With A Handle-Bar Mustache." They cheered "The Boomps-A-Daisy" danced by the chorus and Derby's duet with Steven Kennedy, "I'm Doing It All For Baby." The demand for tickets by soldiers and civilians necessitated an additional week of performances. Eddie sent a pair of ducats to Robert Cadigan, who brought his wife to the show. Eddie constantly did nice things for others, which was one of the many reasons I loved him.

The Lincoln League, a political-action organization, requested entertainment at the club's fiftieth anniversary banquet. The audience of 300 at the Black River Valley Club on Monday, December 14 gave us an ovation for our presentation of the olios. Then it was back to the post for our regular performance. After 26 exciting performances, Derby returned to New York to prepare for our Christmas visit. Major Mason rewarded Eddie and me with ten-day furloughs, "For your hard work and to pick up our plaque," he said. I dreaded that I would have to answer Derby's loaded question, but I realized it was inevitable.

CHAPTER 16

When we arrived at Derby's, she gave me a letter from home. Mother—panicky over the news that Congress had lowered the draft age to 18 and discontinued the parental permission requirement—demanded that I write William and insist that he finish his final semester. I wrote William and kindly asked that he graduate for Mother's sake before he joined the navy. Eddie and I went to the post office on 34th Street and walked uptown to join hundreds of servicemen vying for the bartenders' attention at the overcrowded Astor Bar. I sidled up to a handsome sailor. "Oh, Johnny. What you do to that uniform."

Johnny Miller, *Aquacade* dancer, replied, "Damn, Corporal, you don't look so bad yourself. What's cooking, good looking?" I invited him to Derby's party. "Later? I'm waiting for my ballet partner at Radio City and two shipmates to get out of the movies." I told him to bring them, too.

When we returned to the hotel, Helen Rogers was positioned in the lobby directing Derby's guests. She laughed and told us that she never knew who to expect at Derby's parties. "I'm sending everybody up who looks as if they might be fun." Friends and strangers—every imaginable age, weight, color and social position—mingled, drank and laughed like revelers at Times Square on New Year's Eve. Johnny and his friends arrived. His dancing partner Joan McCracken, whom Derby knew from the Canteen, was no bigger than a minute and cute as red shoes. She had Bette Davis eyes and a radiant smile; all by herself she was a spotlight! She bubbled with the enthusiasm that only a performer hired for a Broadway debut can approximate. She had a contract as featured dancer in the first Rodgers and Hammerstein collaboration, *Away We Go!,* scheduled to premiere in March.

At two a.m., Eddie went with Johnny to see Joan home while his shipmates and I crashed. After 45 minutes of zzz's, we joined Eddie and Johnny at the 123 Club on 54th Street for last call. Then it was back to our room for fraternization. Five horny, inebriated young men and two double beds were the ideal ingredients for a Bacchanalian festival. In a few short weeks, I graduated from menage à trois to menage à cinq.

CBS executives honored us with a luncheon and gave us a recording of our radio show on a set of four 12-inch 78s. Harry Salter presented the plaque which named our "Cheers From The Camps" broadcast as outstanding segment of the series. Writer John Lund, who had just opened in *New Faces of 1943* at the Ritz Theatre, donated four tickets to the hit revue. After the performance, Edie Groome Leach—whose husband was stationed somewhere in the south Pacific—Derby, Eddie and I went backstage to meet John's wife and co-star, Marie Charton. They invited us to their apartment where we spent several happy hours sipping cocktails and talking shop. On the way home, Derby remarked that she thought John would make it big in the movies, which he did the next year.

Derby resumed her duties at the Canteen when she returned from Pine Camp. Eddie and I visited her at work. She looked adorable in her Junior Hostess uniform. She introduced us to many of her co-workers, including Shirley Booth, star of the hit comedy, *My Sister Eileen*. During her turn on stage, Miss Booth sang "Tangerine" and "Kiss The Boys Good-bye." Eddie and I both danced with the future mega-star, who—according to Derby—appeared nightly at the Canteen. The promise of excellent entertainment, good grub and gorgeous girls lured thousands of servicemen to the Canteen seven nights a week. They got good food and good entertainment but not the pretty girls. The hostesses were forbidden to date the GIs or to give their numbers or addresses. No liquor was served at the sanitized nightclub. It was very innocent and sweet. Gay servicemen flocked to the Canteen. Sergeant Merle Miller, *Yank* editor, said, "...my favorite rendezvous was always the Stage Door Canteen. Notorious, Brunhilde. Every time I got off the train I headed for the Canteen. You couldn't go out with the hostesses, but who wanted to? We went out with each other."

Derby read an article about the gifts American admirers sent British Prime Minister Winston Churchill, which included such diverse items as a set of Indian arrowheads, a copy of George Washington's will, a corncob pipe, a Shriner's hat and a turkey wishbone—the "V" for Victory symbol. She duplicated Mr. Churchill's boon and dubbed it her "Prime Minister Christmas." When we opened presents, Derby said, "I wonder who helped Sir Winston unwrap all his gifts?"

"Fala and Faye Emerson," Eddie quipped, referring to the President's prized pet and his movie-star daughter-in-law. "Churchill's spending the holidays with the Roosevelt family."

"How blessed we are to have brilliant leaders who admire and trust each other," Helen said. "Especially at this crucial time. It's very comforting."

In one day we saw six theatrical giants; a matinee of *The Pirate* with Alfred Lunt and Lynn Fontanne and the evening performance of *The Three Sisters* starring Katherine Cornell, Judith Anderson and Ruth Gordan plus Kirk Douglas. *Star-Spangled Rhythm* was a hooty flick. Betty Hutton was terrific; Veronica Lake, Dorothy Lamour, Paulette Goddard and their male imitators camped outrageously; but, we felt our rendition of the George S. Kaufman one-act, *If Men Played Cards As Women Do*, was funnier than the filmed version. Vocalist Frank Sinatra and the Benny Goodman Band were the Paramount stage show. The screaming bobbysoxers swooned when the skinny baritone crooned. Girls literally collapsed in the aisles and were carried from the theatre on stretchers. We marveled at such out-of-control adoration.

We made a special trip to The Dizzy Club to tell Stephen about our successful revival of *She Gave Them All She Had*; however, we were a month late. The draft had snatched Stephen in November.

We went to a slew of New Year's Eve parties, so Derby decided to host a small New Year's Day dinner for our last night of furlough. "Just leave it to me. It'll be fun, I promise." She phoned at three and requested that we bring the recording of the radio program to cocktails. We joined Edie and Derby's family for the first pitcher of martinis at five. Soon Minelda Lange and her fiancé arrived. I was genuinely happy to see her. Minelda's declaration about Eddie and me resulted from her concern for Derby; it was not an attempt to malign us. I liked Minelda. She was a good actress, and we enjoyed working with her.

An hour later, when there was a tap at the door, Derby said, "Tyler, answer that. It's for you." I opened the door to face *Lieutenant* Anthony LaPolla and Helen Luca. Helen had called Derby to exchange season's greetings. When Derby told her that we were staying at the hotel, Helen suggested a surprise visit. Boy, we were three happily surprised GIs!

Eddie shouted above the joyful racket, "Poppy, I'm glad to see you, but let's not make a production of it; just say a few thousand words." Poppy was stationed in Alabama. He looked great and he was happy.

He loved flying. He related some of the problems encountered by the pilot-training program. Many of the bright young men selected for flight school did well in the classroom but experienced severe difficulties in the air. Poppy theorized that it took more than a high IQ to navigate a plane successfully.

Even with wartime rationing, Derby managed a magnificent supper. Poppy had missed both broadcasts of "Cheers From The Camps" due to night-flight duty. He delighted in hearing his Pine Camp cohorts. In between sides, we recalled favorite memories such as Dudley Gilbert falling in Black River, Kimo winning all our money shooting craps when we were supposed to be on a 25-mile field hike, and Minelda limping across stage on a broken heel while Poppy struggled to keep from breaking up.

"Poppy, what do you think of Southern hospitality?" Eddie asked.

"I like the food, and the people are nice; but, they have some weird ideas, especially about Negroes. Some of our best pilots are colored airmen."

"I can't defend my home folk," I responded. "Many of them are living in the last century. They don't know Abraham Lincoln freed the slaves."

"Thank God, the theatrical profession doesn't discriminate," Derby said. "We welcome Negro servicemen at the Canteen. Separate army units, indeed."

"On a lighter note, let me insert a non-discriminating joke," Eddie suggested. "A Negro troop train, passing through North Carolina late at night, was scheduled to stop briefly to pick up supplies. Many colored girls, decked out in their finery, waited at the station in the wee small hours to greet the Negro soldiers. When the train stopped, one white officer got off. The girls couldn't see who was aboard because of the blackout windows. They were puzzled. Finally, one girl timidly approached the white soldier. 'Scuse me, mister. Ain't this a colored troop train?' The white GI looked disdainfully at the colored girl and said, 'I'm a white sergeant, but I've got black privates.' The Negro girl hesitated, grinned, and then said, 'Oo, oo! Ain't you the fancy one!'"

The festive reunion with so many who were vitally important to us during 1942 served as a reminder of the good reasons our country was at war. For a little while, we experienced peace in our hearts, and it made us more determined to do our part to help restore peace on earth.

CHAPTER 17

When we returned from leave in the early morning hours, Monday, January 3, 1943, I found Phil Johnson's note. "Shipped out with Sascha London and Joe Glider. Don't know where. Keep up the good work. I'll be in touch." Our designer/stage manager/choreographer, conductor and best sax player gone, damn. After reveille I went to Kermit Schafer for an explanation.

"They're not the only ones," Kermit declared. "Kimo Dennis, Chet Cooper and Lenny Kane are gone, too." When I asked why, Kermit told me that all post headquarters companies were being reassigned. "Our guys are being sent to redistribution centers to join units headed overseas."

I met with Major Mason after chow. "Corporal, I knew how you would take it, so I sent you and Fuller on furlough because I didn't want to witness your disappointment."

"Major, I can't believe that just when we have a strong entertainment unit in tact, the army is willy-nilly breaking us up. It doesn't make sense. Why can't the 1209th join a Special Service Company?"

"The few existing Special Service outfits are overseas. The War Department is dragging its feet. Red tape, you know the army. A group of officers just entered a Special Services training program at Washington and Lee University down in Virginia. New units will be formed eventually, but not right now. By the way, I will be leaving for overseas in a few days." The sky had fallen. I had to prevent separation from Eddie. I'm certain Major Mason understood my concern. He assured me that he would do his best to keep the nucleus of an entertainment unit together. I had done my best. We just had to wait it out.

The second bomb landed square on me the next day at mail call. Derby wrote, "I love you and I want to be your wife." She assured me that my attachment to Eddie made no difference. She vowed that if I married her "in name only," she could accept the situation. "If I don't hear from you in the next few weeks," she concluded, "I will understand that you think it best to remain single, but always remember that I love you."

At mess, Eddie watched me dawdling over my food. "Lost your taste for army chow?" he asked. I explained that I was thinking about the future. "I know you're worried. We all are, but you'll work it out," he said. I wanted to tell him about Derby's letter, but I couldn't betray her confidence.

Derby really loved me. If I married her, I would not have to worry about exposure. I loved Derby. Occasionally when we petted, I got aroused, but I never tried anything, because nice girls didn't have premarital sex and nice boys weren't supposed to pressure their sweethearts. I liked Derby's family. I enjoyed being included in the Rogers' inner circle. They were glamorous, sophisticated New Yorkers, like the characters I admired in the movies. The family money would provide a security I had never known. Darling Derby, so pretty, funny and fey, needed and deserved a vital lover. She would make a terrific wife, but I would make a pathetic husband. She would grow to hate me. It would be unforgivable to ruin her life to mask my homosexuality. If I married Derby, our marriage could wreck three lives. I loved Eddie Fuller. He helped me to accept and appreciate myself. He meant more to me than anything else. No amount of money was equal to our partnership. We were bonded for life. It would break his heart if I married. The decision made itself.

On the day Major Mason departed Pine Camp, he called me to his office. "Don't worry, Corporal. I've taken care of you and Fuller. I can't tell you where you'll be going because the orders haven't come through yet, but they will. When you get there, tell them who you are and what you've done. Give 'em some good shows. We all need more laughter and music in our lives." We shook hands. He continued, "Son, you did some damn fine work for me, and I'm really proud of you. When you get overseas, look me up."

I wanted to hug and kiss the Major to show my appreciation and affection, but like Belle Watling, reckoned that "it wouldn't be fittin'." I offered a brief thanks, saluted and left.

CHAPTER 18

On Wednesday night, January 20, amid a violent snowstorm, Eddie, Dudley Gilbert, Steven Kennedy and I loaded our gear and waved goodbye to the few members of the 1209th who were still awaiting reassignment. It saddened me to leave them and the rustic Theatre Workshop building that had been my home for the past year. I loved my tenure at Pine Camp.

Thirty-six hours later, the troop train deposited us at Camp Butner, North Carolina, a redistribution center operated by the 78th Lightning Division. The four of us stuck together to maintain our unit identity. When we reached our assigned barracks, I told the guys to get some sleep while I checked out the situation. At Post Headquarters, I requested to see the captain of our outfit. Since it was still half an hour before reveille, I had to wait. When I was presented to Captain Short, I told him that I had produced stage and radio programs at Pine Camp. I gave a brief description of our theatrical credits. "Three of my most talented men are with me. We can present a good variety show on a minute's notice." He explained that General Parker wanted entertainment on the post. He directed me to see Colonel Huntley, the General's morale officer.

While I waited three hours for the Colonel, a young clerk took pity on me and provided coffee and donuts to quell my rumbling stomach. In the Colonel's office at last, I praised my troupe of strolling players to the man on whom our fate depended. Finally, he said, "Well, we'll see what you can do. The Catholic High School in Raleigh is having a midterm graduation dance tonight. They requested entertainment. This might work out for you. You do comedy, don't you?"

"Do anything, sir," I enthusiastically replied. "We know exactly what to offer the high school kids. We'll serve the 78th Lightning Division well." Then he asked for names so that he could put a hold on us until permanent assignments could be effected. I got back to the guys at mid-day. They were jubilant that our beachhead was established.

Colonel Huntley gave us a jeep, a reservation at the Carolina Hotel near the school and 48-hour passes. We arrived at the gym in time for a run-through. Two days after our Pine Camp departure, we were again on stage doing skits and songs. The priests, nuns and parents liked us, but the kids went wild. After the show, we feasted on a lot of good Southern cooking, and we danced with the girls who had no dates since their boyfriends had left school for military service.

Saturday morning we splurged on big Southern breakfasts. Grits were a novelty for the Yankee boys. Eddie and Dudley ordered seconds. We enjoyed the mild North Carolina weather, which was 70 degrees warmer than New York. We visited the Capitol grounds and checked on movie schedules. Steven and Dudley decided on *Star Spangled Rhythm* for the filmed version of the skit we presented the night before. Eddie and I chose the Bogart-Bergman film, *Casablanca*.

We quickly discovered that Raleigh was not the subdued capital city it appeared to be. On our way to the movies, we stopped at the crowded Trailways Bus Station. We could hardly believe the extensive cruising or glory-hole action in the men's room. A nice-looking civilian gave Eddie the eye when he stood at the urinal. Eddie talked to him. We had heard rumors about police entrapment of gay soldiers; consequently, Eddie worked out a routine to proceed cautiously with soldiers and civilians who acted too friendly too quickly. After shooting the bull for 15 minutes, Eddie decided that Stan March, a journalist from Ohio, was okay. Stan announced that he was on his way to meet a soldier from his hometown at the movies. His friend was Private Eddie Malanowski, the young clerk who had kindly given me coffee and donuts. If the film hadn't been so good, we might have done some "feeling up" in the darkened theatre. Over two hot dogs, "all the way," and beers in a tavern, we decided *Casablanca* was an instant classic. The finale innuendo delighted our gay sense of humor. Stan invited us to his place for a party. Eddie and I chipped in three dollars for a bottle of scotch at a state package store, the only place in dry North Carolina to buy booze. Eddie M. and Stan bought bourbon and gin.

Stan lived in the heart of the city in a caretaker's cottage hidden among foliage in the rear of an old mansion. He dubbed his place "The Villa." Stan's guests included sailors, marines and GIs of various rank. To the uninitiated it looked like any bunch of servicemen getting drunk, talking about military life and telling jokes. "When Little Audrey saw a man in the park hugging a tree, Little Audrey just laughed and laughed because she knew that only God can make a tree." Between drinks, a couple of guys would disappear for a while, return, and others would disappear. Everybody was "dropping their laundry" as many times as they were able. Eddie and I fit right in with the group. It was a good, clean orgy which was still going strong when we threw in the sponge about 3:00 a.m.

We explained our long absence to Steven and Dudley with a white lie. We told them we had met a couple of WACS at the movies. We didn't like to be dishonest with our mates, but they were straight. Despite how close we felt to them, we didn't jeopardize our good working relationship. We needed them, and they needed us.

CHAPTER 19

Colonel Huntley received glowing reports on our Raleigh show, and he immediately issued orders to assign us to the 78th in different battalions. I joined a cannon company as acting drill sergeant and operator of a half track, a heavy-duty vehicle with a mounted cannon. Eddie and Steven, assigned to an infantry company, trained recruits and maintained the Rec Hall, where we were allotted space for auditions and rehearsals. Dudley received a desk job in administrative headquarters.

Colonel Huntley's major task was to calm the natives' apprehensions about the influx of military personnel. Thousands of soldiers arrived each week, were processed and shipped out. I auditioned GIs with performing talents and we kept the men suitable for our many projects. The Colonel scheduled us to perform for civic groups at least three nights a week. He gave us a half-hour radio show which aired twice a week on Durham station, WDNC. I did the host duties and introduced a new singer on each program. We offered skits and poetry readings. We often used local female talent. It was simple but fun. General Parker thought it was the greatest so the Colonel was happy. Corporal Harold Ray, a terrific juggler, tumbler and comic, was in charge of the Rec Hall. Harold lived off base with his wife, a very good singer and darling "ball of fire." We cast them in many skits and they toured with us for stage performances all over the area. Captain Ralph Roberts, an assistant to the colonel in Post Headquarters, was our biggest fan and ardent supporter. Captain Roberts had decided to become an actor, and he wanted to know all about our pre-army stage and radio jobs. We entertained in the evenings while on maneuvers with our respective companies. Eddie, Steven and Dudley were true blue during this period of triple duty. We wanted to stay together as long as possible and realized that our existence as a unit depended on quality shows.

In late March, Eddie and I wrangled three-day passes so that he could meet my family before we shipped overseas. "Extra-curricular" action on the Jacksonville train, filled to the gills with servicemen, kept every men's room constantly packed. Eddie shielded a sailor and me on the platform between cars from the sight of passing conductors and milling passengers.

My brother Edward was home on leave prior to shipping overseas, and my cousin Ben Ewing came up from Orlando. The three younger boys were home on Easter break. Mother was in her element with seven guys on the premises. She used all her ration points and borrowed stamps from relatives to ensure that her boys had some favorite dishes. We took Mother dining and dancing at the Roosevelt Hotel. Pat and Buddy were underage and not allowed in places that served alcoholic beverages. About midway through the evening, they made a surprise appearance. Buddy used his gift of gab to convince the doorman to let them join their brothers in uniform. Buddy and Eddie became great pals. The return trip was an uneventful Sunday night ride for us because we were bushed, but for others it was hot-to-trot action as usual.

Colonel Huntley lined up three major stage projects during our absence: a variety show starring the Ritz Brothers, a fundraising revue for the Raleigh Junior Woman's Club to support student nurses in training for war work and a "Womanless Wedding" for the Red Cross Recreation Center at the Camp Butner Post Hospital. We busted butt getting two revues staged simultaneously. The Ritz Brothers wowed the soldier audience. Babs Butner, radio star, sang and played straightman for the Hollywood zanies. Singer Myrt Alexander was a big hit as was husband Harold's juggling act. Sergeant Max Bernstein dazzled the men with his Carmen Miranda imitation. The Dotson Brothers from the Negro 530th Q.M. Battalion, known professionally as The Hottentots, tapped to big rounds of applause. The Division Artillery dance orchestra supplied the music. Dudley emceed and acted with Harold, Eddie and me in our standby, *If Men Played Cards*.... For the variety show, we cast 35 soldiers including Corporal Bill Mata, brother of film star Private Desi Arnaz. Bill played classical guitar and sang. Eddie and Private Roy DeWitt wrote several new songs including the hit, "Doughboy Doakes." The show raised thousands for the nursing program.

I tore cartilage in my knee during tank maneuvers and was sidelined for several weeks. The supply sergeant asked me to be his assistant so I transferred from the cannon company to supply. The change gave me more time to develop entertainment projects, plus I had my own jeep. While I was hobbling about, Private Ralph Burgess directed the "Womanless Wedding." Eddie emceed and cast ten husky, butch types for what was basically a drag show. Pure unadulterated camp barely describes the ridiculous extravaganza which provided lots of laughs for the bed-ridden soldiers and sailors.

Canteen dances were held at the Service Club on Friday nights. Girls from neighboring towns, transported by army truck, arrived to dance and socialize with the GIs. There were 50 guys for each girl and the stag lines were lengthy. Gay and bi-sexual soldiers soon discovered that the stag lines were an excellent opportunity to make contact with guys who wanted some action. During the early hours of darkness, the stag lines grew progressively shorter as handsome soldiers sauntered to the enormous drill field across from the Service Club where many men, as anonymous shadows, enjoyed sex under the stars. Eddie and I met lots of guys, including officers on the drill field where many gay friendships and love affairs began during canteen dances.

Despite the many demands on our time, Eddie and I went to Raleigh occasionally for the perpetual open house at Stan's villa. Lots of the boys who frequented the villa parties were not gay. They were lonely GIs uncertain of the future. The prevailing "eat-drink-and-be-merry" attitude of the times prompted them to throw caution to the wind. "When soldiers get whoozy, they forget to be choosy," or do they? A group of ten to 20 gay non-coms—masculine enough not to attract attention—met at the Service Club at ten each morning. We joined them when we could, and they gave us suggestions for innovative activities. The Service Club was rarely used in the evenings except on Friday nights for Canteen dances. We revived our Pine Camp success, *Let's Have Fun!*, on Wednesday nights. The rapid turnover guaranteed a fresh audience every other week. Our old stuff was new to them. The guys loved live entertainment, and we packed 'em in. I asked Lieutenant Claus, the Post Exchange officer, whether we could establish a beer garden to accommodate the overflow. He got permission from General Parker, and by midsummer there were a half dozen beer gardens on the post. We rotated live shows among the beer gardens which also had juke boxes, and we kept our steady pace of radio programs and performances in school auditoriums over a 50-mile radius. We heard rumors that Special Service Units were being formed for overseas assignment. Eddie and I wanted to join one, but nobody at Butner had any information. We figured we were doomed to hang in with the 78th as long as possible, but the ax fell in July.

CHAPTER 20

When the 78th Lightning Division went on maneuvers in July, I was in charge of supplying water to the many companies. We started delivering drums of water at daybreak. At 10:00 a.m. I gave the men a break. One day while we were resting in the shade, my assistant said, "Oh, shit. Here comes the Major." This major had a reputation for being a hard-nosed, by-the-book officer. When the private asked whether we ought to look like we're doing something, I told him not to sweat it. I assured him that a break was legit. When the Major reached us, I called attention.

"Corporal, why aren't these men working?" the Major demanded.

"It's time for their break, sir."

"Has all the water been delivered on time?" he bellowed. I told him that it had.

"Well, I don't know about that. I just came by Company C and they were under the impression that the water should have been there 30 minutes earlier than you delivered it." I responded that we had followed the schedule. "All right," the Major continued, "let's go over there and find out about the discrepancy between what they say and your opinion. We can walk through the woods." When we were out of earshot of my men, the Major said, "Which way is Company C's headquarters?"

"I went by jeep before, sir. I'm not sure but I think it must be straight ahead." After 15 minutes of aimless wandering, the Major sarcastically told me to follow him and led me out of the woods which he clearly resented. After another fifteen minutes, we reached our destination.

The Major strutted to the Captain's tent. He said, "Captain, didn't you tell me your water was delivered late?"

"Yes, sir," the Captain answered, "but we didn't have any problems." The Major repeated his question and intimidated the Captain into saying what he wanted to hear.

"I thought that was the situation," the Major said. "Corporal, find your own way back," he ordered, accompanied by a snort of disgust.

The following day I was relieved of duty and busted. I returned to camp for reassignment. I went ape with worry. Eddie and Steven were in the field with their company. Dudley and Colonel Huntley were on leave. I sought help from Captain Roberts, our stage-struck friend, in Post Headquarters. I explained my plight. "You're some hot potato, now, but I'll speak to my Colonel," he said.

When Captain Roberts returned, he said, "The Colonel will see you. Tell him the complete truth. He's a good man and can be trusted to do the right thing." After I offered the details of my dilemma, the Colonel told me that he would investigate the situation and that I should return to his office the next morning. I was sick with worry; separation from Eddie was almost a reality. I might not even get a chance to see him before I shipped out. I went to our little office area in the Rec Hall and prayed.

After a sleepless night, I double-timed it over to Post Headquarters. Captain Roberts greeted me with a smile and a cheery hello. He placed his hand on my shoulder and did a Gabriel Heatter imitation. "'There's good news, tonight!' Orders just came through from Fort Meade requesting the immediate transfers of Corporal Carpenter and PFC Fuller to the 34th Special Service Company."

"It's a miracle; it's what I've been praying for," I gasped. "My God, how did it happen?"

"Don't question it. Here are the orders and the Colonel honored them without delay because the request was made prior to your problem." He paused. "Would you like a few days leave in New York while your transfers are being effected?" the Captain asked. I nodded an agreeable yes. "I think I'll join you," Captain Roberts continued, "I've never seen a Broadway play."

The Major who busted me stormed out of the Colonel's office. He put on a show for my benefit and I enjoyed his performance. "What the hell is happening? We'll never win the freaking war if we give fancy-pants actors preferential treatment," he ranted like a lunatic. "He's getting transferred with his sidekick and his rank restored. Something's rotten and it ain't in Denmark; it's here, Goddamn it." None of us knew what had happened, but for once I didn't question an army decision.

The next morning Eddie and I departed. Since we didn't get a chance to tell them good-bye, Eddie left a long farewell letter for Steven and Dudley in which he expressed our genuine affection, gratitude and best wishes.

CHAPTER 21

Derby was so excited that Eddie and I were assigned to a Special Service Company where, unfettered, we could do the work we did best: put on shows. I don't know how Derby explained our romantic breakup to her family, but they were as cordial as ever.

When Captain Roberts arrived several days later, we immersed our friend in the New York we loved. We saw Miriam Hopkins' exciting performance in the Pulitzer-Prize winning drama, *The Skin of Our Teeth*. Rumors that its celebrated author, Thornton Wilder, was "in the club" had circulated in New York for years. Now as Major Wilder, he did intelligence work for the Army Air Corps. Margaret Sullavan beguiled us in *The Voice of the Turtle*. Joan McCracken's show underwent a title change during its out-of-town tryout. Joan was a minor Broadway celebrity as a result of her non-speaking role as "the little girl who falls down" in *Oklahoma*, which was hailed by the critics as the hit of the century.

At the Canteen, Joan soberly told us that her dancer-husband, Jack Dunphy, had been drafted, but she bubbled with good news about her contract to appear in the film *Hollywood Canteen* and her co-starring role in *Bloomer Girl* on Broadway. When Eddie asked her how it felt to be a movie star, she joked, "Phooey, Louie on that. I just want to meet Bette Davis." June Havoc, star of *Mexican Hayride*, jitterbugged with a thrilled Captain Roberts.

When the Canteen closed, I walked Derby home. She suggested we join the crowd on the steps of the library on Fifth Avenue for a cigarette. Derby believed it was socially okay for a woman to smoke in public if she were seated. We chatted about her radio and modeling work. Eventually, she discussed the war. She wanted my opinion on how much longer it would last. Now that we were on the offensive, I gave her an optimistic reply. "The Allies have Rommel on the run in Africa, and our men just chased the Japs out of the Aleutians. I'll be home next year as a civilian in time to vote for FDR."

"Oh, Tyler. I hope so."

Two Negro soldiers were seated on my right. The guy next to me said, "Excuse me, buddy. Have you got an extra light?" I gave him a pack of matches. We talked. They were Southern boys, too. We shared where we'd been stationed and what training had been like. We discussed the war news. They told us they'd been to Harlem, their first time in a nightclub. Derby suggested they visit the Canteen. They thanked her but explained that they had to report to the Brooklyn Navy Yard at 0600. All the men in their outfit had been given 24 hour passes; they expected to ship out in a few days. We exchanged good luck wishes and left. "They were nice boys, Tyler. I really don't understand how our government justifies blatant racist treatment of colored soldiers. It's so unfair."

"I know. Maybe it will change after the war. That's part of the liberty we're fighting for. At least President and Mrs. Roosevelt think it is."

"God bless Eleanor and Franklin," Derby sighed.

Helen Rogers showered Captain Roberts with bags of snacks and magazines when he boarded at Penn Station. "It was the greatest time of my life," he shouted. "I love New York and I want to be in a Broadway show."

"Don't we all?" Derby exclaimed. "And we will. A whole bunch of them and together."

On our final night of leave, Eddie and I were at Derby's having farewell drinks and listening to the radio. Derby received a call. "Where are you?" we heard her ask. "Wonderful.... Tyler and Eddie are here.... Come at once. We'll be waiting." She flashed her very best dazzling ingenue smile. "That, my darlings, was *Captain* Anthony LaPolla. He'll be in on the next train from Jersey."

"Oo, oo, Captain LaPolla, ain't you the fancy one!" Eddie said when Poppy arrived at midnight. Poppy was on a two-day layover before going overseas. He looked tired but handsome as always.

"Do you know where?" Derby asked and then corrected herself, "but, of course, you can't say."

"Yeah, 'Loose Lips Sink Ships,' but I expect to join two million GIs already over there," Poppy smiled and winked.

"No crystal ball is needed to predict that your menu offers mutton and plum pudding instead of turkey and fruitcake this Christmas," Derby said.

We told him about our transfer. "It sure saved my butt. And now the chance to see you. How lucky can you get in this man's army?"

"Actually, I had planned to call Derby in the morning. Divine intervention, I suppose," he said and threw his hands heavenward. "Thank you, Lord."

Like groups of Americans throughout the nation, we talked about current events such as Axis Sally's broadcasts, "Germany Calling." The propaganda queen exaggerated American losses and used the contents of captured mail to accomplish her demoralizing dirty work. "I read that the war is costing the country 90 billion a year," Poppy stated. "I didn't think there was that much money in the world." We spoke of the many wartime creations: 92-percent employment for both men and women, Japanese-American detention camps, meatless Tuesdays, rationing, five-minute limits on long-distance calls and shared taxis. We discussed the Polio epidemic, the Detroit race riots, the Yankees' chances for a pennant and the B-29 Superfortress. Poppy jokingly boasted that when he flew a B-29 over Berlin, "Watch out, Adolf. The war will be over by Christmas."

At two a.m. we each gave Derby hugs and kisses. "Take care, my dearest ones," she said between tears. "The next time you see me, I promise to have mastered the technique of getting my hair to fall over my eye à la Veronica. Happy landings!" She quickly closed the door.

We grabbed a shared taxi uptown to Reds, a gay bar at 52nd Street under the El. "Whatever," was Poppy's motto. With so many uniforms about, Reds looked like any neighborhood bar. We spent two hours swigging beers, catching up and swapping jokes. "When Little Audrey heard that the Marines were stationed in the Virgin Islands, Little Audrey just laughed and laughed because she knew that the Navy had already been there." Eddie knew hundreds of Little Audrey jokes.

Eddie gave Poppy some snapshots of us taken on leave in Jacksonville. "Helen and I had photographs made today. I'll have her send you one," Poppy promised. Servicemen always exchanged pictures with buddies. We wanted to ensure our immortality. When Poppy departed, he hugged Eddie and me. We told him how much we treasured his friendship. "Ditto," he said and smiled. "See ya." We watched him walk west on 52nd Street until he was out of sight.

CHAPTER 22

While Eddie and I waited at Penn Station for a 10:00 a.m. train to Maryland, I went to the men's room. When I descended the second flight of stairs, I saw servicemen and civilians engaging in sex on the stairs, at the urinals and in the booths. Incredible but true, as I pissed, I noted a poster on the far wall: "Flies Spread Disease—Keep Yours Buttoned."

We solved the riddle of our transfers when Second Lieutenant Dennis, our buddy Kimo who'd performed in every play we staged at Pine Camp, greeted us. When Kimo left Pine Camp, he went to OCS. "Captain Fletcher doesn't know shit from Shinola about show business. I told Lieutenant Nash that you two guys could get this company together in a flash. He gave permission, so I traced you to Butner and did the paper work. Hot damn, I'm glad to see you."

Kimo didn't exaggerate; the company was a disaster. Captain Fletcher had a Master's Degree in Fine Arts; but he was a scholar, not a performer. Eddie and I were the only professional actors in the show platoon. We coached the musicians to read lines and taught them several dance routines. In a few days, we developed a decent variety show.

August was bivouac month for the 34th. Our introduction to pup tent life and chiggers in the woods adjacent to the Annapolis Roads Country Club was followed by maneuvers on balmy Chesapeake Bay, where we went sailing and swimming in our free time. I was "in like Flynn" with Captain Fletcher because I could operate every piece of heavy-duty equipment and artillery. He ignored my theatrical skills, but he ate up my combat abilities.

Hollywood star Sabu, the elephant boy, was assigned to the 35th Special Service Company which didn't know how to use his talents. I asked the Captain to get him for our outfit, but Fletcher denied my request. Sabu transferred to the Air Corps where he earned many decorations as a tail gunner. I hated to let a major talent we needed get away.

Washington was Wildsville, USA! During blackouts, its many small parks teemed with straight and gay action. Gay GIs flocked to the men's bars in the Mayflower and Statler hotels, The Chicken Hut and Carroll's Opera House. Civilians at the bars often issued invitations to house parties; there were more than a few "villas" in D.C.

The D.C. Stage Door Canteen needed performers. The Canteen director was delighted when we volunteered. I approached Captain Fletcher as if the Canteen had initiated a request for a weekly performance. He reluctantly agreed. Our debut was a hit. The Captain enjoyed the praise and confirmed our future appearances. Comedian Jackie Mason, the headliner our first night, sang "Honeysuckle Rose" and camped outrageously. The GIs went wild when he sat in a sailor's lap.

Fort Meade had a radio station, FGGM. I went through a similar routine to get us on the airwaves. After I gave the Colonel in charge a run-down of our experience, he requested us to do two shows a week. Captain Fletcher reluctantly complied.

We worked harder than ever on field training. I put the men through hell. We dug fox-holes. We repeatedly crawled over the infamous infiltration course where we endured lots of barbed-wire scratches but no machine-gun casualties. We marched, marched and marched some more. One of Eddie's pet expressions was, "Do we have to do that, AGAIN? Now, isn't that the *silliest* thing?" The men in the show platoon recognized that I was trying to please the Captain, and they cooperated.

Nineteen-year-old Private Harry Kerovitz, assigned to our platoon as a cook's helper and PX worker, joined the newspaper staff. He and Eddie collaborated on several articles, and Eddie became his hero. "Where are you from?" Eddie asked the young soldier. "I know it's some place where watermelon is a menu staple."

"Louisiana," he laughed and slapped his leg.

"That's too many syllables. I'll just call you Dixie."

Captain Fletcher served as advisor to the newspaper. He interpreted advisor to mean censor and the *Cadence* staff resented his tight-assed policies. "I don't like the Captain," Dixie told Eddie. "He treats me like change from a nickel."

"Listen, little buddy," Eddie cautioned, "be careful. As the poster says, 'The Walls Have Ears.' He's got a few stooges. We're all sick of his 'just two more items' routine, but what you say has a way of getting back to him. Then, it's hell to pay for everyone."

We were by far the most visible Special Service Company in the area, so the War Department selected us to represent Special Services at the huge army display staged to support the 4th War Loan Drive. Four officers and 85 men went to Washington on August 30. All divisions of the military were represented by individual companies quartered in tents on scenic Hains Point alongside the Potomac. We spent ten days setting up our exhibits in two carnival tents and eight adjacent outdoor displays on the Washington Monument grounds.

The "Back the Attack 4th War Bond Drive" opened with a magnificent parade. President Roosevelt, accompanied by Greer Garson—*Mrs. Miniver* herself—rode in the lead car followed by thousands of soldiers, sailors and marines passing in review. Fifty major Hollywood stars including Judy Garland, Hedy Lamarr, Abbott and Costello (the President's favorites), Marsha Hunt (a personal favorite), the Andrews Sisters et al. rode in open cars and later auctioned bonds. We performed on our portable stage at the base of the Lincoln Memorial as if we were appearing for troops in the field. Massive crowds turned out for our six shows a day. Also we continued the Canteen shows and radio programs.

The exhibits closed at 8:00 p.m. to observe blackout regulations. Our nights on pass perplexed Captain Fletcher. He hated that we were having so much fun. He treated us as if we were front-line troops during our entire Hains Point encampment. Every member of the company bitched about reveille with a bugle when no other outfit required it. The Captain's "brown nosers" snooped and reported on us constantly. Rumors reached us that Mrs. Roosevelt ate supper on the south porch of the White House so that she could watch our show while she dined and that she had sent compliments to the Captain.

During a typical bull session, Eddie—the instigator—said, "Dixie, how could you be so disrespectful to Mrs. Roosevelt?" Dixie looked puzzled. "I heard that she inspected the kitchen when you were making decorative designs on cookies by slapping the balls of dough in your navel before you popped them in the oven. Eleanor said, 'Oh, how clever.' And you said, 'Lady, that ain't nothing. You shoulda been here yesterday; I made donuts.'" Two days later at reveille, Captain Fletcher told us that contrary to rumor, Mrs. Roosevelt had not visited the camp. He'd swallowed the bait which amused us to no end.

The term SNAFU—Situation Normal, All Fouled Up—described all kinds of military mishaps until the term FUBAR—Fucked Up Beyond All Recognition—replaced it. One night the Captain restricted us to the area. "Pretend you're in a war zone and create your own entertainment. Sit around the campfire and sing a few songs," he commanded. Everyone bitched.

"This is the fucking end."

"I'll bet that bastard puts his pants on to answer the telephone."

"Up his giggy with a meat hook."

"My nuts could bust before I'd let that SOB peel my eel."

I finally blurted out, "Shut up. He's just a Two-Bar FUBAR. Sing some songs to please the asshole, and let's get some sack time."

Several mornings later at reveille, we stood at attention in a light mist while the Captain silently paced and gave us a thorough going-over. Finally, he spoke. "This company had better toe the line from here on out. I've heard about Two-Bar FUBAR."

CHAPTER 23

We felt good about our part in "Back the Attack." Visitors purchased double the bond-drive goal. The show platoon jelled. Eddie and I both tried to convince the Captain that we were ready to mount a company show. "We're needed as a fighting unit overseas," he responded. "The invasion will require combat-ready soldiers. We'll entertain on the side and send the guitar players to the front lines. We won't need a big show." His reaction appalled us. He had no concept of the function of Special Services. Indeed, we were infantry-trained, but our first duty was entertainment. Captain Fletcher wanted to lead a fighting unit, and he had decided that the 34th Special Service Company would be it.

Our outfit received more publicity than the other Special Service units at Meade, and envious members of the other units razzed us. One of Two-Bar FUBAR's stooges reported the slander. Scuttlebutt was that our company got the lion's share of recognition because there were more queers in the 34th. The Captain went ape. All enlisted personnel were called into headquarters for a probing one-on-one interview with FUBAR. "Corporal, when men function in an all-male environment, sometimes personal attachments get out of control. I will not tolerate unnatural acts between the men in my company. I insist that my men be good soldiers and a credit to their uniforms."

"Captain Fletcher," I said, "since May, 1941 my primary objective has been to be a good soldier. Sir, I am the best drill sergeant in the outfit, which I have proved on many occasions. I am a good soldier and I will continue to be a good soldier." He dismissed me from the interview with a salute. I promised myself that I would show Two-Bar FUBAR how a good soldier behaved. I drilled the men with extra target practice, bayonet charges and obstacle courses until the show platoon was as well-trained and competent as any outfit in the army.

Kimo invited Eddie and me to go to Washington on pass. He told us that he was transferring to a Special Service Company in California. "I don't want to go overseas with Two-Bar FUBAR. I apologize for getting you hooked up with him. I thought I was doing the best thing for you and the company," Kimo said and took a deep drag on his cigarette. "The Captain doesn't like me because I refused to be a stoolie. Also I petitioned him to allow you to stage a company show. You shoulda heard the shit he threw at me. 'I'm in charge of this company. If I can't trust my own lieutenant, who can I trust?' Jaw, jaw, jaw! I guess Major Mason and Major Blesser spoiled me for all other leadership."

We lost our major ally and a true-blue buddy; however, we kept working on a major show. I felt so frustrated. The show platoon expected me to wheedle consent from the Captain, and I was powerless. Eddie kept calm and advised me to do the same. He was my rock. We tried out our new material in our Canteen appearances and on the radio program. Thank God, the Captain was unable to find a legitimate reason to discontinue those activities.

Corporal Phil Dickinson, *Cadence* editor, printed General Eisenhower's remarks to the cast of a Special Service revue in North Africa: "You are not fighting with machine-guns, but your job is just as important...You are rendering a service, and a great one, to your fellow soldiers and your country." We expected the Captain to react, but he did not comment on the article.

In November the men took turns going on furlough. We were certain we were only days away from shipping out. Eddie and I were not eligible for leave. Everyone returned by Thanksgiving on November 25. We had a holiday party in a gaily decorated mess hall. All of our equipment was packed in waterproof cases, so we knew we'd spend Christmas over there. Corporal George Riggs wrote an editorial for the Thanksgiving edition of *Cadence* which expressed what every man in the company wanted to say to the Captain: "...Special Service's mission is to carry across to our boys, as they come out of the trenches, a program of Entertainment, Education and Recreation which will help them forget the horrors of what they are experiencing and keep them in touch with that part of the world they are fighting to preserve." Riggs waved the red flag, and the bull attacked. Captain Fletcher busted Riggs and transferred him to the motion picture division. Two-Bar FUBAR summoned me to his office.

"Carpenter, I'm going to transfer you to another Special Service Company and keep Fuller. You two guys have been together too long and think too much alike."

"Holy shit," I thought, "the asshole is going to destroy me." I wanted to hurl invectives; instead, I gave a performance. "Captain Fletcher, sir, I know you have good reasons for your decision, but please reconsider. Obviously, we are shipping out in a few days, and if you replace me now, it will mean breaking in somebody new at the 11th hour." I continued apace. "I work well with the men. I have developed a number of good friendships. I believe that the outstanding reputation of the 34th will be eroded if you break up the theatrical section now. I pledge that the men in the show platoon will always be combat ready." And then I played my ace. "I'm the best man in the company with explosives and canons. When we get to the front lines, you will need me, sir."

He bought my spiel. Two days later, we boarded a troop train which deposited us at Camp Shanks in Orangeburg, New York, 20 miles north of Manhattan. We endured a final week of processing, which included showdown inspections, more physical checkups, more shots, abandonship drill and the routine 25-mile hike with fieldpacks.

Everyone received a 12-hour pass for a final stateside spree on the town. Eddie visited Edie. I went to see Derby. We agreed to rendezvous for dinner at Pat's on West 45th Street, where I'd been a waiter.

As soon as Derby saw me she said, "It's overseas, now, isn't it?" I nodded yes. "Let's have a martini and you tell me what you can."

While we sipped a lot of good gin, Derby told me that she had met someone. "His name is Robert Wilcox. He's an actor, God love him, and a soldier. RKO Pictures was grooming him for stardom when he was drafted. He's had small parts in ten films. He's 29, very handsome and sweet. I know that you and Eddie will like Bob. He shipped out last week; England, we think."

I hugged Derby. "Darling girl, I'm so happy for you. If you love Bob, then I'm sure Eddie and I will, too."

"I have your present from Poppy," she said as she handed me the portrait. "Helen Luca delivered it last week. We had a good visit. She loves Poppy more than she loves life. He's stationed north of London, which is all she can tell from his letters." We chatted on through the afternoon. I told her about Two-Bar FUBAR and how frustrated we were. Derby commiserated with our plight and offered encouraging words. "Keep your chin up, dear. I liked Morris Rosenberg," she continued, "it must be fun to work with him."

"We call him Rosie. He's a hoot and a great entertainer. He told us about his appearance at the Canteen," I responded.

"The audience loved his Helen Morgan impersonation. Carole Landis presented him with an elegant shaving kit. Ty, I want you to meet Carole. She is so funny and beautiful. I think she sings and dances much better than Betty Grable."

As we walked uptown, Derby offered ebullient chatter about anything and everything to avoid the topic of my departure. "My diction teacher William Eythe has a Fox contract. He's made three films in six months. He's a wonderful actor. Watch out for him. He's 4-F, the poor darling. His eardrum was damaged during a fight scene on stage in *The Moon Is Down*. Shirley Booth asks about you all the time. She sang 'Skylark' on Thursday night. There wasn't a dry eye in the Canteen."

Edie and Eddie were waiting for us. After a long, happy evening of cocktails and dinner, the girls walked with us to the Bus Station on West 50th Street where we shared another moist-eyed farewell. "Write, please, write!" Derby shouted as the bus pulled out of the terminal.

CHAPTER 24

At midnight on Saturday, December 4, 1943, we rode a train to Weehawken and then a ferry across the Hudson to the Cunard White Star Pier. We joined thousands of servicemen standing in line. Eddie and Dixie swapped Little Audrey jokes. "Little Audrey went swimming in the harbor and banged her head on a big ship. Little Audrey just laughed and laughed because she was used to hardships."

"Have you heard this one? 'When the sailor told his mother he joined the navy to see the world, Little Audrey just laughed and laughed because she knew that boys joined the navy to ride the WAVES.'"

An army band played "Hail, Hail, the Gang's All Here" as the 34th Special Service Company—five officers and 109 enlisted men—filed up the gangplank and into the deep, dark hold of the HMS Britannic. We descended narrow stairs in pitch blackness until we reached bottom where we crawled over sleeping bodies. An unseen stranger bellowed, "Find a space and sack out."

Nine thousand men stood on deck that Sunday morning when the renovated luxury liner passed the Statue of Liberty. The silence penetrated the soul. You could read the prayers in the men's eyes. "Dear God, please let me come back."

Out on the vast, gray Atlantic, other ships joined the convoy. We had our first lifeboat drill. Phil Dickinson said, "This is no dry run." With nothing to cushion motion down in hold E-6, most of the men were seasick, including me. At daylight each morning, Eddie and I went on deck so that I could jog, breathe deep and lose the dry heaves. The two meals a day were skimpy and typical examples of bad British cooking. Eddie slept on a table where we ate. As cook's helper, Dixie had access to the kitchen. He provided us with extra food which I couldn't eat. Several times Eddie said, "If it weren't for Dixie, I'd starve to death."

The days were long. On our third day out, Axis Sally announced that U-boats had sunk the Britannic. Thank God, no one knew what ship we were on. We never sighted an enemy vessel, but the inevitable rumors of German subs stimulated our imaginations. About mid-ocean, Captain Fletcher finally distributed the booklet, *Guide to Britain*, which confirmed what everybody already knew. Navy projectionists ran films day and night, but the lines were so long that many of us never saw a movie. We watched the other ships roll through the heavy swells. We sang to amuse ourselves and waited in line to buy cigarettes and candy at the canteen. We planned the company musical. Eddie revised the lyrics of "Stars Without Garters."

> We're stars without garters; elastic's no more
> We're stars without garters; we're just rubber poor.
> Our Uncle Sam gave us an outfit sweet
> Hats for heads and shoes for our feet.
> But no substitute is forthcoming yet
> To take up the slack in our drooping anklet.
> Our dress uniform is strictly Esquire.
> We're soldiers of fashion, we don't mind the ration.
> It's good for the passion, you bet!

Two-Bar FUBAR got a taste of what was expected of Special Services when the ship's Captain demanded that we perform. The bands staged jam sessions on every deck and in the hold. We presented a variety show in the main dining salon. The newspaper staff published a daily which introduced a new cartoon, "Private Pokey," created by Corporal Bart Tumey. "Private Pokey" was picked up by *Yank* and eventually syndicated in civilian papers.

The ship's rest rooms had peepholes in all the booths and bath stalls. Everywhere you looked, guys dated "Lady Five Fingers." The Staff Sergeant I had met at the Jacksonville "Y" in 1942 joined Eddie and me for a salt water bath. Going to the head provided many good laughs and lots of relief.

A couple of land-based planes circled overhead on the ninth day, and the next morning we glimpsed the northern tip of Ireland on the starboard side. We crossed the Irish Sea on the 11th day and sailed into the Mersey River estuary where we anchored in a pea-soup fog shrouding Liverpool.

We filed down the gangway in drizzling rain on December 17. I lost 15 pounds during the crossing. I was as limp as a dishrag. PFC Teddy Breitenfeldt, one of the smallest men in the outfit, asked, "Ty, why are you lagging behind?"

I looked at the steep, red-brick ramp leading to the railway platform. "I can't get myself and my duffel bag up that long, slick incline."

"You can do it, pal. Come on," he said. And that little mite of a soldier took my duffel bag and slung it over his shoulder with his own.

American Red Cross workers greeted us with coffee and donuts in the station. We boarded dimly-lit, six-seater railway carriages with blackout blinds. We slept during the ride to Bristol, where English ladies served tea and cakes. Then we piled on another train. It was nine a.m. and still dark when we arrived at our post—drab, muddy Camp Boreham.

As soon as we were settled, I told Eddie that we needed to put together a Christmas show. He promptly produced a script, *Dust of the Road*, about a miser struggling with his conscience on Christmas Eve. We needed an actress to play the wife and a girl singer to provide an angelic aura. I commandeered a jeep to go to the women's barracks of the British Air Force 12 miles away. The WAAF officers were delighted to be invited to join a Yank show. They introduced us to a darling singer named Mary Simm and her actress friend, Beryl Weir. In several days, we were audience ready.

Christmas day was cold and wet. Every man was allowed to send one cable to the states. We ate a traditional turkey dinner in the Rec Hall at Tilshead Lodge on Salisbury Plain. After real American apple pie, we presented our show. The play and carols were followed by an upbeat second act of cheerful music featuring our singers and instrumentalists. The program restored the men's morale just like the regimen of three daily meals of good American chow quickly restored our strength. Jewish Dixie quipped, "This is the best Christmas of my life."

Whenever we could escape Captain Fletcher's infantry drills (all of 12 times), we presented performances of our holiday entertainment for the English and American troops stationed in and around Warminster. At each showing, the men clamored for more, and the WAAFs really loved us. Somehow we had to counter Two-Bar FUBAR's objections to a company musical. We knew that the time and place were right for a blockbuster revue.

CHAPTER 25

Incessant rain, fathomless mud, penetrating cold, inadequate heat and few hours of daylight made our first weeks in the United Kingdom a memorable period of adjustment. "Sunshine is a rationed item in England," Eddie mused.

We exchanged Yankee dollars for pounds sterling. The men quickly grasped the value of exchange when Dixie lost 20 pounds in a crap game before he realized he had shot 80 bucks. We willy-nilly mastered British denominations such as bobs, guineas, florins and quids, but we rapidly calculated that half-a-crown—the price of two beers and a pack of crisps (potato chips)—was in the neighborhood of 50 cents.

English lingo required attention. Torch for flashlight; lorry for truck; spanner for wrench; fag for cigarette; and knock you up for wake you. We soon learned that the British expression "keep your pecker up" meant stay cheerful, but it provided a lot of giggles.

We were lucky to get a hot shower every third day. The English adamantly demanded the conservation of fresh, hot water since it required rationed fuel to operate pumps and geysers (water heaters). Posters in the latrines announced, "Switched on lights and turned on taps, Make happy Huns and joyful Japs." We washed and shaved in rainwater heated on stoves in the barracks. We tamed the lye-based GI soap by mixing in generous portions of hand cream. We could buy most items in the PX, but at times good soap was in short supply.

We were introduced to local fare in the quaint village of Tilshead. We liked fish 'n' chips liberally sprinkled with vinegar and salt and pints of mild 'n' bitter, a warm, tan brew less filling than American beer and more potent.

U.S. Armed Forces Radio—coordinated by Majors Tom Lewis and Harry Salter, civilian speakers at the 1942 Special Service planning conference—eased our culture shock. The 24 hour broadcasts maintained

U.S. schedules, so we laughed at the antics of Jack Benny at 7:30 on Sunday evenings just as if we were at home.

The enlisted man supposes and occasionally the army disposes to the soldier's advantage. Our heaven-sent opportunity arrived New Year's day. Captain Fletcher received orders to report to London for a three-day conference of company commanders. As soon as Two-Bar FUBAR departed, I rushed to Lieutenant Nash's office. I requested permission to stage a company show in Captain Fletcher's absence. Lieutenant Nash said, "Corporal, I have strict orders to follow the training schedule. The Christmas show was great, but you know how the Captain feels. He believes we must focus on being combat-ready and limit live entertainment to band concerts and dance engagements."

"Please give us a chance," I pleaded. "We will mount the show on our time. We've got the talent. Private Fuller's got the scripts. We can be audience-ready before the Captain returns. The time is right for a company show. I swear to maintain the training schedule."

"Carpenter, I admire your determination. Okay, let's see what you can come up with; but, don't foul up the training schedule."

I called the show platoon together. I explained the conditions: three days on our own time to mount a company show. Nobody complained. We rehearsed and drilled, and drilled and rehearsed. Dixie and Teddy Chapman, company clerk, typed as Eddie dictated topical revisions. Dixie said it was like a Judy Garland-Mickey Rooney musical when the kids put on a show in the barn and end up on Broadway. Like Little Audrey, Dixie just laughed and laughed.

The WAAFs were happy to be our premiere audience. The cast included PFCs Harold Baymiller, George A. Breitenfeldt, Thomas Clemente, Lucien F. Irena, Robert F. Kane, Michael J. Florio, George Miller, Waldo E. Proctor, Charles Raphael and Dominick Santoro; T/5s Teddy B. Chapman, Charles D. Chamison, William S. Irena, Herbert Dell, Joseph M. Lutz, Johnny Romano, Morris Rosenberg, Roger A. Sullivan and Alfred K. Toplis; and T/4 Arthur S. Ryerson, Jr. conducted the orchestra. T/4 Alger C. Mason and PFC Albert Dannibale handled tech.

When we gathered on stage for final details, Eddie concluded with, "Two-Bar FUBAR, Sirrrrrrrrr! Here comes the best damn company of players you'll ever see in an unforgettable evening of superior theatre."

I added, "Keep your peckers up and keep your powder dry."

We did it. The WAAFs squealed with delight at each of the ten segments. The next day we gave two performances for American battalions, and the third day we gave back-to-back performances for the British Air Force. They repeatedly cheered, "Hip, hip, hurrah!" Lieutenant Nash strutted like a peacock and basked in the glory of our success.

When Captain Fletcher returned, he met with the entire company. We expected severe rebuke. Instead, he informed us that General Eisenhower had issued orders that all members of Special Services, including cooks and mechanics, be trained projectionists to meet the demand for motion pictures made by the three million Americans stationed in Great Britain. When President Roosevelt asked Ike what he needed most, the General replied, "Send us more movies."

Two-Bar FUBAR found his desk heaped with congratulatory letters and requests for *Stars Without Garters*, but he did not discuss the show with any cast member. He honored the requests, but he never attended a performance. During the first three weeks in January, we gave 23 shows to an estimated audience of 18,700 appreciative GIs, Tommies and WAAFs.

Private John R. Bucklin from Marblehead, Massachusetts instructed me in film operation. Short, dumpy Johnny wore thick, wire-rimmed glasses which enlarged his already over-sized blue eyes that naturally rolled and fluttered. He looked exactly like actress Laura Hope Crews who played Aunt Pittypat in *Gone With The Wind*. He was a hoot and as gay as pink ink. He wasn't swishy or obvious, but we read each other's tea leaves and became good buddies. We shared many pleasant hours laughing at Abbott and Costello in *Who Done It?* and the equally funny Carmen Miranda and Charlotte Greenwood in *The Gang's All Here*. Eddie and I suspected that several guys in the 34th were gay, but John was the only one we confided in. We felt it best to keep work and play separate.

CHAPTER 26

When we received orders to move south, we suspected that the imminent invasion of France beckoned and that Two-Bar FUBAR had volunteered us to spearhead the attack. Long before the cock crowed on January 26, 1944, we loaded for the junket to Sussex. We hurried up and waited for hours in heavy rain for daylight. I drove the truck which hauled our portable stage, sound system, piano and other instruments. Eddie rode shotgun. We were positioned last in the convoy.

While we were waiting, Dixie emerged from the weapons carrier in front. He hustled to the passenger side of our vehicle and jumped in. Eddie spouted a favorite GI greeting, "Hey, Joe. Whata ya know?"

"Guys, listen. I just made up a Little Audrey Joke. 'When Little Audrey's mother told her that women cross their legs when they sit down so men can't see their underwear, Little Audrey just laughed and laughed because she knew she wasn't wearing any panties.'"

We laughed and laughed. Dixie beamed. Eddie said, "I've been wondering who's responsible for the proliferation of Little Audrey jokes. Now, I know. You are." Dixie slapped his leg in his unique Southern-boy way and erupted with gales of infectious chuckles. "Dixie, you've got the happiest, healthiest laugh of anybody I know."

"As my 'ole mammy use to say, 'Laughter is the best medicine for what ails you.' I ain't exactly khaki-wacky for the army, but I sure do dig the GI jive. See you at chow. Roger, Wilco, and out." Dixie returned to his transport and sat on the end. He saluted and we saluted back.

The rain let up, but the heavy mist impaired visibility. The narrow, muddy roads—designed for horse and wagon—forced us to travel at a snail's pace. The cavernous ruts cut by the heavy vehicles made the ride rough. At Stonehenge, the fog miraculously lifted. We gawked at the ancient ceremonial ruin in the middle of a pasture where sleek Holsteins grazed contentedly among the giant monoliths. "I hope we get on a paved road soon. This bumpy ride is like being back in the hold of the Britannic," I complained. Just then the truck in front bounced skyward. A soldier flew out and up and plummeted to the ground like a rag doll. I slammed on brakes.

"Sweet Jesus," Eddie yelled, "it's Dixie!"

Johnny Bucklin leaped from the victim's slow-moving truck amid a roar of shouting voices. "Stop! Damn it, stop!"

"Stop, there's been an accident!"

"Halt, for God's sake, stop!"

Johnny sped to Dixie's side. We sprinted to the edge of the muddy road where Dixie lay perfectly still. Bucklin examined him. "No pulse. No heartbeat."

"Breathe, Dixie, breathe," Eddie stammered.

"He can't, Fuller. He's dead," Bucklin stated. "His neck is broken."

"Nooooooo!" Eddie wailed. "Oh, God, no. Please don't let it be." Eddie cradled Dixie's head against his chest and wept plaintively. "My buddy. My dear, funny, little buddy." He closed Dixie's eyes and wiped the mud from his face. He unbuttoned Dixie's shirt and inserted the dead boy's dog tags between his teeth the way we had been taught. I watched Eddie holding the young soldier until I could not bear to view his grief any longer. I walked to the far side of our truck and cried.

A Red Cross ambulance arrived 30 minutes later. Eddie helped the women lift Dixie's body onto a stretcher and place it in the van. They drove away. Eddie stood beside our truck. He sobbed and shook. Then he heaved and vomited. I tried to comfort him. "My dearest one. I am so sorry."

We had not seen action, but we had trod the path to death when Private Harry Kerovitz, age 19, died tragically on Salisbury Plain in the shadow of Stonehenge.

CHAPTER 27

We delighted in our elegant new quarters four miles east of the quaint village of Petworth. Phil Dickinson said, "Out of this world for an Army billet." Burton Park House—a three-story mansion built in 1828—offered such non-military adornments as a marble assembly hall where we stood reveille; a grand staircase with a bronze balustrade; eight steam-heated bathrooms; a walnut-paneled library; and marble washstands and fireplaces in each squad room! Burton had a small chapel with an ancestral graveyard dating to the 16th century. Surrounding the manor house and church were spacious lawns with aged ilex and elm trees, paved walks and a flagstone terrace overlooking a formal rose garden and lily pools. Inviting paths led to several lakes and rhododendron thickets with forests beyond. Our luxurious abode dazzled us, but we met the challenge. We played softball on the lawns, volleyball on the tennis courts and handball on the indoor squash court.

Some of the guys bitched that the English were rude and unappreciative. A favorite expression—"The Yanks are overpaid, overfed, oversexed and over here"—rankled the guys who also bristled at the phrase, "How green was my ally," which referred to the invasion of North Africa. The men failed to appreciate British humor. "Did you hear the one about the two Yanks who went to a war film? One fainted and the other one got a medal for carrying him out." Our platoon leaders conducted weekly orientation meetings to dispel ignorant ill feelings. Our guys grew fond of the English when they met the hospitable and amusing local residents at the Cricketer's Inn, a pub a mile from the mansion in the tiny hamlet of Duncton. We liked the pints of bitter, dart games and cozy seats inside the enormous fireplace. Eddie made friends with a 92-year-old Mr. Fuller and his son, Constable Fuller, who was the entire Duncton police force.

Most combat units trained seven days a week for seven straight weeks during which time the men were confined to their posts; consequently, requests for live shows, films, athletic equipment and reading materials skyrocketed. Captain Fletcher sent us on endless marches through the lush countryside to neighboring villages tucked along the edges of the South Downs. Teddy Chapman, the company clerk, informed us that Two-Bar FUBAR often ignored requests for *Stars Without Garters* if the bookings interfered with his training schedule. "I want soldiers, not actors, with me in France," he said repeatedly. He really planned for us to meet the enemy head on. If any of us survived, then we could entertain and sing while we victoriously marched through the streets of Berlin. Again we were thwarted in our attempts to fulfill the function of Special Services. Obviously, something had to be done about the lunatic.

Major James Mason, our Pine Camp leader, headed Special Services in the northeastern region; we were located in the southeastern district. Since I could not place a phone call through the military hookup, I called him from the Cricketer's. I explained our genuine concerns. "Captain Fletcher not only denies requests for the company show, but he ignores requests for films, concerts, etc. if the requests conflict with his training schedule. He does not allow us to do our jobs." Major Mason accepted my complaints because he knew I would not fabricate such serious accusations. The Major assured me that he would relay the information to headquarters in London. Two days later, Captain Fletcher was summoned to London. Lieutenant Nash honored the stockpile of requests for our show and accelerated all other functions.

On March 2, 1944, we listened to the Academy Awards Ceremony—broadcast for the first time—on Armed Forces Radio. We were delighted that Jennifer Jones, nee Phylis Walker, won an Oscar for *The Song of Bernadette*. The GIs liked the religious film that co-starred William Eythe, Derby's handsome diction teacher. We knew the Walkers and had seen them in several plays. I appeared with Robert Walker on two radio soaps, "Myrt and Marge," and "John's Other Wife" in 1940.

When Captain Fletcher returned, he met with the cast. He explained that performances would be given in the p.m. and that we must return by 2300 hours. Chapman told us that Two-Bar FUBAR's eyes bulged and his face turned crimson when he checked the schedule we had maintained in his absence. "They've been going out all along, and I'm doing everything I can do to stop this," he said. "Something's happening here that I don't understand."

Often it was impossible to return by the designated time. If we gave a second or third performance, we did not return until 0100. Two-Bar FUBAR did not give us credit for the hard work and long hours we put in. And it was hard work to load up, drive to the location, set up the portable stage, give a performance or several, strike the set, load for the return, and drive back to Burton Park in total blackness. Plus we still had to stand reveille at 0600, attend to regular duties, occasionally show films, and combat train prior to preparation for an evening performance. Lieutenant Nash understood. He insisted that we take off every fifth night. Captain Fletcher was heard to say, "If they're so damn dedicated, why do they have to take off so many nights." FUBAR was angered and frustrated by his obvious lack of control.

One "free" evening, Eddie came to my room. "Tyler, I need to speak to you in private. Let's go to the library."

Something told me not to blurt out, "Why now, when everyone is lining up for chow?" I followed him up the grand staircase and across the enormous room to the ceiling-high windows which overlooked the garden. Gigantic bolts of lightning zig-zagged across the lawn and illuminated the roses and lily pads like klieg lights at a Hollywood premiere. Eddie gave me a letter in Mother's florid penmanship which explained that my 17-year-old brother, Buddy, had been killed in a boot camp accident in Beaufort, South Carolina. Mother asked Eddie to break the news to me. I was stunned. I did not know that Buddy had joined the navy during the Christmas holidays. I thought he was still in school. Eddie held me close while I cried. The news of Buddy's death revealed anew the significance of Eddie's and my relationship. We were there for each other. Eddie had told Lieutenant Nash about Buddy's death, and the Lieutenant alerted the men. As they left the mess hall, each man silently patted my shoulder or nodded. After chow, we went to the Cricketer's Inn. Bill Irena, a macho Italian kid from Brooklyn, gave me a warm embrace. Then he put his arm around his brother Lucien and kissed his cheek. "Little brothers are a pain in the ass sometimes, but we love 'em anyway," he said.

Soldiers seldom spoke of death. We knew that thousands died daily, but we did not discuss it. Once the ambulance departed with Dixie's body, we did not mention his death. One morning Eddie and I were clowning as we loaded the truck. Eddie said very softly, "I miss Dixie's laughter." Eddie never told another Little Audrey joke.

I wrote Mother and told her to stop feeling guilty that she had signed the consent for Buddy to join the navy. He believed it was his duty to enlist. Her response, a month later, asked me to send the bad news to Edward, stationed in the south Pacific. Poor Mother, with four sons in the service, never knew a minute's peace during the war years. I sent Edward a V-mail. In another month, I received his reply. Well, thank God, Edward was alive.

Captain Fletcher continued his policy of 25-mile hikes with full equipment, which often resulted in canceled performances. Whenever we got wind of the situation early in the day, either Eddie or I rushed to the Cricketer's and called Major Mason. Once Teddy Chapman called Major Mason for us because Two-Bar FUBAR had Eddie and me on special detail in his office under his watchful eye. Several times when he thought he had us in a bind, FUBAR received calls from London requesting confirmation of our appearance that night. He became greatly agitated by the many requests for the show platoon to demonstrate Special Service functions at officers' orientation meetings in Bournemouth. The stress showed in his appearance and behavior. He lost weight and his skin turned gray. He raved like a maniac at the slightest provocation. Captain Fletcher was frantic.

General Eisenhower provided us additional ammunition in the personal war between Captain Fletcher and the cast of *Stars Without Garters*. Ike, in a letter dated Sunday, March 5, 1944 addressed "To Every American Serving Under My Command," wrote, "Recreation and entertainment are necessary for soldiers in the ETO. Company commanders...should make it possible to attend plays, movies and lectures as well as to accept privately offered hospitality...."

Major Smythe, the chief of Special Services throughout England, came to Burton Park for a conference with Captain Fletcher and the platoon leaders. Three days later on March 21, Two-Bar FUBAR was transferred to a scouting position at the Western Base Section and advanced in rank. As far as we knew, Major Fletcher never learned why he lost his position as Company Commander of the 34th.

Lieutenant Nash was promoted to captain. Lieutenant Robinson became our platoon leader. I finally received my sergeant stripes, and Eddie made corporal. The entire outfit went on a binge the likes of which had never been witnessed at the Cricketer's Inn. The joint was jumping. Boy, did we sling the slang! Hubba, hubba! Bing-bam-boff-zowie! Well, all reet, Mellorooney!

Dixie would have loved it.

CHAPTER 28

Captain Nash rewarded each member of the company with monthly (retroactive) 48-hour passes. Most of the men hopped the train to London and cavorted in the world's largest city. Eddie read in *Stars and Stripes* about a theatre symposium at Stratford-upon-Avon for enlisted men. Our accumulated leave entitled us to ten-day furloughs for a combined trip to Stratford and London.

We hitchhiked. Englishmen who owned cars rarely drove due to gas rationing; consequently, we depended on military transport. We rode on a supply truck from Petworth to Bath where we spent the night. The ancient innkeeper provided an elegant room furnished with antiques. He supplied a hot water bottle and a pot of strong tea to combat the unheated, damp quarters where we nearly froze in medieval comfort. The large featherbed, piled high with quilts so heavy that it was nearly impossible to move, lured us like the song of the sirens. It had been months since we slept together. Two WREN (British Navy Women) officers gave us a lift to their barracks north of Bath. From there we hiked along country roads where we viewed the mating of a bull and heifer engineered by two elderly farmers, who employed a rope and stick to guide the bull. I thought we would see a production, as I assumed that the mounted bull would snort and hump for an extended period. To my dismay, it was "slam, bam, without even a thank you, ma'am" and over in less than a minute. Damn, talk about being shortchanged! A handsome Captain from Montana gave us a long jeep ride to Honeyborne. We passed acres of daffodils; bolts of radiant yellows gleamed so bright they stunned our eyes and illuminated the drab day. The Captain treated us to a tongue sandwich and beers at a country pub. In Evesharn, rain forced us to seek refuge at the Red Cross Club where a Miss Fuller from Massachusetts served us coffee and donuts while our clothes dried.

We arrived in Stratford at dusk. England had just adopted Double Summertime, a ploy to aid production, and it did not get dark until 10:30 p.m. Stratford's cobblestone streets were filled with American soldiers who gaped at the centuries-old houses with crooked brick walls and wooden timbers.

The three-day course was even better than we had anticipated. All of the actors were cordial; Patricia Jessel, who played Lady MacBeth and Katherine the Shrew, had us to tea twice in her dressing room. We were thrilled by a superior production of *A Midsummer Night's Dream*. Mary Honer, a star of the Sadler Wells Ballet, was the finest imaginable Puck. John Byron, also a former ballet dancer, played Oberon. Their fluid movements created genuine excitement. We also liked Mr. Byron's Hamlet, but Eddie said that it didn't compare with the John Gielgud production he had seen in New York. A footnote in the playbill stated: "Director Robert Atkins apologizes for the drastic cutting of *Hamlet* made necessary by the time-limit imposed by traffic restrictions." We joined the ladies in the audience who emitted audible sighs of desire for Mr. Byron in tights.

We visited Mrs. Whittfield with whom Eddie roomed in 1935. She was so glad to see him that she served her last jar of pre-war preserves—magnificent gooseberry and strawberry jam flavored with elderberry syrup—and idiot biscuits, so called she said, "because they are so simple, any idiot can make them." Eddie gave the Whittfields some of the PX items—Spam, fruit cocktail and chocolate bars—that we had stashed in our duffel bags to repay kind hosts.

RAF pilot David Halliwell, whom we had met when we performed at his base in Wiltshire, joined us for an overnight visit and an amusing production of Ben Johnson's *Volpone*. When David could not find a room, Eddie asked Mrs. Whittfield to house him. She readily opened her home to David and graciously served him breakfast even though everyone in England suffered from short rations. When David attempted to pay her for the kindness, she said she would be insulted if he didn't stop such nonsense.

David's apple-cheek freshness was more pretty than handsome, and he was utterly charming and polite in the best public school-boy tradition. After the theatre, we scoured the crowded streets for a safe haven where we could satisfy our carnal cravings. The three of us finally settled on the banks of the Avon under a weeping willow where we sipped apricot brandy and lollygagged until dark. Lovely "double summertime" inspired the rhyme: "This British time is an awful crime. What good is a park, if it ain't dark?" Each time David climaxed, he announced the event in passionate, audible gasps, "I'm going to spunk, I'm going to spunk." I added some essential British lingo to my vocabulary under that willow tree in Stratford.

At Anne Hathaway's thatched-roof cottage, I was thrilled to sit on the well-worn bench where William Shakespeare courted his wife. The cottage garden filled with peonies, roses and tulips, and the apple orchard beyond were majestic. David, Eddie and I danced and sang "Don't Sit Under the Apple Tree" beneath the blossom-laden boughs. We were young and gay, and we were so pleased to be who we were and where we were. As Gertrude Stein wrote, "Everything was wonderful...and we knew it was wonderful every minute it was being wonderful...."

CHAPTER 29

We arrived at congested Victoria Station in late afternoon and taxied to the Howard Hotel in the heart of London's theatre district where Eric Portman, Eddie's friend and a star at Stratford in 1935, had made our reservations. Thousands of GIs strolled the streets. Quentin Crisp described it beautifully:

> The American forces...flowed through the streets...like cream on strawberries, like melted butter on green peas. Labeled 'with love from Uncle Sam' and packaged in uniforms so tight that in them their owners could fight for nothing but their honour...their bodies bulged through every straining khaki fibre.... The liberality of their natures...was so marvelous. Never in the history of sex was so much offered to so many by so few.

When we entered the hotel, a smiling Lieutenant rushed across the crowded lobby and grabbed my hand. "Tyler, Bill Irvin from Tallahassee," he said. "Gee whiz, it's good to see somebody from home." Instead of the little freckled kid I remembered, I faced a handsome officer. We visited amid the commotion while Eddie checked in. Bill invited us for drinks, but we had theatre tickets. We deposited our duffel bags in the room and dashed to the Duchess Theatre to see Noel Coward's hit comedy, *Blithe Spirit*.

Actress Moya Nugent honored us with house seats to the popular farce. Mr. Coward wrote the role of the doctor's wife for Moya, which she played brilliantly for the full six-year run. Though never a big star, Moya was an accomplished comedienne and always worked. In 1934 she created the role of Brat in Coward's *Tonight At 8:30* in New York. She and Eddie became bosom buddies. For the next five years, she appeared on Broadway in a series of hits. When the war broke out,

Moya felt it her patriotic duty to return to England.

We loved the play. At 11:00 p.m. Eric Portman arrived from Canterbury where he was completing exteriors for the film, *A Canterbury Tale*. "My dear boy," Eric greeted Eddie. "How I wish you were playing the Yank in this picture. You would be smashing as the GI. I am beside myself. The film is scheduled to open in ten days, and we still have several principal sequences to shoot. War shortages, you know. C'est la guerre. C'est la vie. It's a nightmare." After champagne with Moya's co-stars, Eric led us to his limousine surrounded by a hoard of adoring fans desiring autographs. Charming Eric obliged his public while Moya, Eddie and I piled into his stately car. He waved to the crowd and we were off. He took us to a chic, after-hours gay club, Le Boeuf sur le Toit—The Bull on the Roof—for members only. Champagne and martinis were plentiful, but the food offerings were meager. Nobody complained. "There's a war on, you know."

"Dear boys, I am coming in to the West End in a modern piece, *Zero Hour* at the Duke of York's in May," Eric told us. "I will reclaim my home which is on loan to ENSA (Entertainment National Service Association—the British equivalent of the USO). On your next leave in London, I insist that you stay with me." Well, there we were! Two Yanks receiving royal treatment from Britain's number one film star of 1943 and a co-star of the hit play of the decade, the war magically vanished.

"I'll introduce you to Lilian Braithwaite at lunch on Friday," Moya said. "She's very fond of handsome soldiers, especially if they're actors." Eric delivered us to the hotel about 3:00 a.m. and dropped Moya on his return to Canterbury.

Wise Dr. Samuel Johnson wrote, "When a man is tired of London, he is tired of life; for there is in London all that life can afford." We visited St. Paul's, Westminster Abbey, Buckingham Palace, the Tower of London, Dr. Johnson's home and his favorite tavern, The Cheshire Cheese. We shopped at Harrod's and like everyone else pretended not to notice that the great food hall had no merchandise. We passed Temple Church and refused to gape at the bomb damage. We marveled at the small red flower, London Pride, which sprang up out of the rubble. The little red blossom was unknown before the blitz. Noel Coward wrote a song about the phenomenon.

We enjoyed people, plays and pubs. Helen Rogers' retired friend, Colonel Lionel Spencer, entertained us at the exclusive Officer's Club.

He was a delightful old gentleman who introduced us to many of his WW I buddies. While we drank and swapped war stories, time slipped away, and we had to forego the formal dinner the Colonel had planned at Simpson's. Instead the three of us gobbled fish 'n' chips in a taxi on our way to the Strand Theatre to see Dame Lilian Braithwaite in *Arsenic and Old Lace*. Dame Lilian, knighted in 1943 at age 71, was enjoying the greatest success of her distinguished career. At the end of Act I, Eddie said, "Thank God for intermission. One more laugh and I would have wet my pants." When the play ended, we thanked the Colonel for a terrific afternoon and evening.

It was just getting dark at 11:00 p.m. Eddie and I bee-lined it to Le Boeuf sur le Toit where we fell into the midst of a gay, military international party of at least a hundred officers and enlisted men. Hubba, hubba! We drank with the Irish, danced with the Danes and laughed with the Australians until four a.m. We walked to the hotel in complete blackout where we encountered many men and women making out in the entrance ways and small connecting streets. We were groped and propositioned by both sexes, but we were ready for sack time. We were barely asleep when a shower of Hitler's buzz bombs rudely awakened us. Since 1940 the Jerries had attacked London just at 11:00 p.m. Obviously, Adolph didn't know about Double Summertime. From our window we saw six fires; one of them less than a mile away. Our first time under attack was sobering.

We slept till noon. Eddie went to Rainbow Corner, an American Red Cross canteen on the corner at Piccadilly Circus and Shaftesbury Avenue, in search of food. He returned with Major Brutus, a sexy member of the Coldstream Guards. I took one look at the Major's kilts and said, "Oo, oo. Ain't you the fancy one," which prompted Eddie to tell a favorite joke. We spent several hours getting really well-acquainted during which time we solved the riddle of what a Scot wears under his kilts. He wore, as the popular English joke said, "The new utility knickers: one Yank and they're down." Two Yanks and they completely vanished! Later the three of us went in search of libation at a succession of gay pubs in Leicester Square and Soho: The Scotch House, The White Room, The French House and The Captain's Table. At midnight, Major Brutus took us to a rowdy, semi-gay bar, The Klomp Klub, where we purchased memberships for six shillings ($1.20). We fell head-over-heels for the club and its hooty hostess, Dolly. Eventually Major Brutus crashed in our room for a couple of hours before he reported for duty at 0600.

Mid-morning Major Mason's secretary phoned to say that he would meet us at our hotel that afternoon. We taxied to the Ivy Restaurant, London's equivalent of New York's Sardi's. I lugged a shopping bag of PX items which Eddie presented to Moya. Between tears she said, "How utterly smashing of you to shower me with an array of precious gifts." Spam, fruit cocktail, soap, candy and cigarettes—worth about ten dollars—were rationed goods which could not be purchased for love or money except on the Black Market. And no self-respecting Englishman ever traded on the Black Market. "Do tell me all that you have been doing to amuse yourselves," Moya cooed. "Well, maybe not all." Eddie titillated her with an account of our doings which provoked fits of giggles. We enjoyed a hearty lunch of non-rationed oysters, venison roast and ubiquitous sprouts.

At a large table by the entrance, Dame Lilian dined with Hermione Gingold. We fawned over Miss Braithwaite and her performance. She asked many questions about our work. When I told the ladies that Major Mason was joining us, Miss Gingold suggested that we bring him to see her hit revue, *Sweet and Low* at the Ambassador's Theatre. "All the Yanks love it, and I'm sure your Major will, too," she said.

"I work for ENSA," Dame Lilian informed us. "I book hospital shows and I could use you. Also you must meet Bea Lillie. She's booking acts for the opening of the London Stage Door Canteen in September. Give me your commanding officer's name and I will pass it on to Bea." After an hour with the captivating ladies, we took a bus to Kensington Gardens to see the Albert Memorial.

We spent three hours with Major Mason in a pub near the theatre, catching up and reminiscing about Pine Camp days over beers and ploughman's lunches. We gave him heartfelt thanks for his assistance in expediting Two-Bar FUBAR's transfer. "Boys, I trusted your judgment. I knew that you wouldn't ask for help unless it was necessary." We explained that freed of FUBAR we were doing some of our best work. "That's a whole lot of doing, considering the fine shows you did stateside," he said.

Miss Gingold was right. We were three more Yanks who loved her campy revue. Her bow-legged lady cellist had us rolling in the aisles, and the sweetly earnest finale, "Thanks, Yanks!" evoked a few tears. We stopped briefly backstage to pay our respects, and Hermione introduced us to her wonderful second banana, Gretchen Franklin.

The Major treated us to drinks at the Savoy, and then we took him to the Klomp Klub where he flipped over Dolly. We partied for three hours with them before we kissed Dolly and hugged the Major adieu. "Boys, I have a request. Can you get me an autographed picture of film star James Mason to send to my ten-year-old Jimmy, Jr.?"

"Consider it done, Major," Eddie said. "I'll get my friend Eric Portman to handle that request." When we left them, the Major and Dolly were happily swapping World War I memories.

The next morning a couple of tired, hungover, but happy soldiers returned to Petworth by train.

CHAPTER 30

We knew that all operations in Great Britain during the first half of 1944 were aimed exclusively toward the invasion of continental Europe. Two days after we returned from furlough on April 17, our company transferred from Sussex to Dorset to play our part in the crucial project. When we departed Burton House, we were extremely proud that we did not leave a trace of vandalism in the mansion.

Our new post at Dorchester Barracks, HQ for Marshaling Area D, was an old military garrison. Our job was to provide recreation and entertainment to the assault troops in the marshaling areas along the southern coast. The sixteen D camps were hidden in the wooded hills and hollows that divide Dorset and Hampshire and in Southhampton's spacious city parks. All leaves were canceled. Eddie and I were lucky to have completed our Stratford/London excursion before the relocation.

The 34th established recreation centers, libraries and theatres in Nissen huts, mess halls, assembly tents, or whatever could be improvised. In short order, most of our field theatres acquired fancy improvements such as projection booths, sound systems, permanent seats, stages and even dressing rooms in a couple of instances.

"Without movies, I'd go nuts," was a popular sentiment among the assault troops. During the day, we ran movies, movies and more movies. I showed two Betty Hutton features, *And The Angels Sing* and *The Miracle of Morgan's Creek*, at least 25 times each in the same week. To amuse myself, I turned off the sound in the projection booth and recited the lines in sync with the screen action. We distributed newspapers and books by the thousands, ran bingo tournaments and doled out athletic equipment. The demands for recreation kept us hopping. At night we took *Stars Without Garters* to the D camps. We gave performances for French, Turkish, Canadian, British and American troops. Then we were sent out along the entire southern coast. We even performed for General Eisenhower and the top brass at Dover.

Several days after we arrived in Dorset, the bodies of two murdered Negro soldiers were found floating in Weymouth's bay. The variance between most white GIs' amiable dispositions and the discernible contempt for their black comrades puzzled the British. The satirical comment, "I don't mind the Yanks, but I can't say I care for those white chaps they've brought with them," agitated many white GIs. Many of the men were perplexed because the English regarded black GIs as a novelty and genuinely liked America's Negro soldiers. Our platoon leaders exhorted us to avoid all contact with colored servicemen.

One night when we were performing in Hampshire, several Negro soldiers were doing janitorial duties in a room adjoining the backstage area. When the orchestra began the overture, Eddie opened the doors so that the black GIs could watch the show unseen by our all-white audience. On the way back to the post, Eddie commented, "Tyler, the army's treatment of colored GIs is unforgivable." I remembered Derby and the conversation we had with the Negro soldiers on the steps of the New York Public Library. Eddie and Derby really were cut from the same bolt.

The American army made extensive use of zoning which reserved certain towns or individual public houses for the exclusive use of one race or the other. "Blacks, Tuesdays; whites, Wednesdays" was a common arrangement to provide off-post diversion for segregated troops. Gladys Mahoney, a white Alabama native, made mincemeat of the army's divisive zoning system. Gladys, a 40ish widow, operated a bar on the ground level of her home on the outskirts of Weymouth. Gladys had one rule. Everyone was welcome at any time, but all must behave. And we did, blacks and whites together. Gladys Mahoney was a good woman and a pioneer. After a visit to Gladys' our guys stopped yakking about "niggers," and our company did not have a single incident of racial conflict.

Being the ranking senior enlisted man sure came in handy. I had my own jeep. Every fifth night when we were officially free, Eddie and I drove into Weymouth after chow to carouse. Often we met Johnny Bucklin who was on detached service east of Weymouth. One evening Eddie didn't show up at mess. I found him in the barracks. "What's the score?" I asked. "We're supposed to meet Bucklin."

"I'm ready."

"You missed chow. What have you been doing?"

"I finally wrote Dixie's parents."

Bucklin introduced us to the wonderful Kikaldee family who operated Bert's Pub in Weymouth. Mom and Pop Kikaldee tended bar and Sylvia Jean, their 16-year-old daughter, waited tables. Bert's Pub opened at 6:00 p.m.; however, due to the limited supply of beer and the few rationed bottles of gin, Scotch and Pimms to serve hundreds on some evenings, all the booze disappeared by seven. We developed a technique to get a buzz from the limited supply. Buy a beer and pour the allowed one jigger of liquor into the beer. Scotch mixed with beer was decent, but gin combined with beer created a mean beverage that would gag a maggot. The Kikaldees were genuinely cordial and often invited us to their living quarters in back of the pub, where we drank from their private stock. We liked being in a family setting once again, and frequently gave them small items from the PX. Sylvia Jean had a sweet tooth and acted as if we had given her jewels when she received a roll of Life-Savers.

One evening at Bert's, when the crowd was small and the liquor supply lasted for several hours, I noticed a handsome American sailor alone at the bar. I invited Lew Granger to play darts. When the pub closed, Eddie suggested that the three of us tour Weymouth's bombed-out areas. We were clumping around in the rubble and stumbled upon a GI and his girl in the back of a gutted building engaged in heavy-duty sex. We quietly backed away. The sailor asked, "Do you like the English girls?"

"I'm much more interest in you," I replied.

"God, I'm glad," Lew said. "I thought you'd never ask." The three of us found our own wrecked building and engaged in some hot action. Well, all reet! Hubba, hubba!

We became good friends with Lew, and he introduced us to some of his shipmates who were gung-ho to have a good time. The sailors had Torpedo Juice—160-proof alcohol—which they drained from torpedoes and strained through bread to get rid of the chemicals added to make it undrinkable. We always stashed cans of fruit juice in the jeep when we went to Weymouth in case we bumped into Lew and his mates. When we were lucky enough to have liberty on the same nights, they piled in the jeep with us and headed for the woods, where we made cocktails of equal parts Torpedo Juice, fruit juice and water. We imbibed until we were plotzed, and then dropped our laundry. Sensational! The sailors hopped the last launch back to their ship and we returned to D-9 in time for bed check.

On our company's first anniversary as a unit, Captain Nash received a letter of commendation from Colonel Logan C. Berry, commandant of the D Area. "The work of the 34th Special Service Company has set an extremely high standard of recreation and entertainment.... I confidently expect your success to expand and continue as greater demands of the constantly developing situation present themselves...."

Praise from the brass was terrific, but it didn't compare to the joy of running films during the day and traveling at night to present live shows to our most deserving soldiers. Their laughter, cheers and applause were our greatest commendations.

CHAPTER 31

Pop Kikaldee joked, "Do you Yanks carry pleasant weather in your duffel bags?" Frequent short showers coupled with lots of sunshine created an aura of health and hope. The lush vegetation provided a backdrop of pastoral beauty for the million GIs who invaded Dorset in endless convoys. The men admired the fertile acres of barley and wheat dotted with orange poppies and fields carpeted with wine-red heather. The GIs smiled and waved to the natives. When the kids yelled, "Got any gum, chum?" they tossed packs of gum, candy and pocket change. Shillings and pence were passé. The men were already thinking francs. Actually the tension was so thick you could cut it with a knife. Films and stage shows offered respite, and the guys momentarily forgot their eerie feelings of fright at being among the first scheduled to sail to the far shore.

When we showed films, we also played General Eisenhower's recorded pep-talk and ran "Private Snafu Cartoons" which instructed the men in an entertaining way about spies, female-double agents, venereal diseases and damage created by rumor and needless talk. The GIs howled at Private Snafu's risqué antics, but they got the message. We distributed leaflets on France which gave general information and warnings. *Stars and Stripes* offered more practical advice. "Don't be surprised if a Frenchman...kisses you. That doesn't mean he's queer. It means he's emotional, French, and darn glad to see you."

Each time vast columns of men and vehicles moved out, we wondered as they did whether or not it was another "dry run" or at last, "the real thing." Often we got up in the middle of the night to run a movie for an outfit before it moved out, and our theatres were used for last-minute church services. When the real thing occurred on June 6, there was no mistaking it for a dry run. In contrast to the perfect weather all spring, the elements were ominous. Blustery winds, driving rain and choppy channel waters prevailed. The all-night roar of C-47s from Devon flying east told us it was D-Day. For 60 consecutive hours, we trudged along the pebbled beach in blinding rain and distributed books, newspapers and playing cards to the GIs as they boarded landing craft. The men were eager, anxious and scared, but they were so positive that the operation would liberate the world from the heel of Nazism.

In the first 24 hours, 176,000 men went to the far shore in 6,939 naval vessels and 15,040 aircraft. Phil Dickinson called the departure "a never-to-be-forgotten spectacle." The distant sky became violently red, and muffled booms from heavy bombing wafted in from France. The next morning and all that day, boat loads of wounded men returned to Weymouth. Ambulances and trucks transported thousands to the medical trains bound for hospitals in Bournemouth and Blandford. About one man in 11 who landed on D-Day was killed, wounded or missing. And each hour more troops shipped out.

D-Day plus 1 (June 7, 1944) was Eddie's 33rd birthday. When we were finally relieved of duty, we went to Weymouth to celebrate. The streets were deserted. Three American sailors came around a corner. They rushed to us. They embraced us and between sobs began to tell us the horrors they had witnessed. "The guys shot craps, told jokes or read during the crossing. Then an hour later, the nightmare began. You never saw anything like it. You guys are being massacred. We couldn't do anything but look and yell."

"Oh, God. It was horrible and so many. They got bulldozers to scoop up the dead to make room for more to come out of the water."

"They kept trying to scale those God-damned cliffs. I stood there. I just stood there. I wanted to help. I wanted to do something."

"After we unloaded, we pulled out and left all of them there."

"Oh, God, I can't take you over there. No more. No more!"

We tried to comfort them, but they were inconsolable. We took them to Bert's for drinks. Pop Kikaldee handed us a local paper which announced, "Our Troops Are Ashore and Moving Inland." Eddie's birthday was not too festive, but we had lots of drinks and listened to the eyewitness accounts of the landing in Normandy. The harrowing details alarmed us, but they also inspired both mental resolve and emotional stamina to perform our jobs with greater determination. When we passed the statue of Thomas Hardy on Westgate Street in Dorchester, Eddie said, "I wonder what the great scribe would make of the atrocities that now plague his beloved country?"

Several weeks after D-Day, Eddie received a letter from David Halliwell's father. Our beautiful, apple-cheeked, charming RAF pilot had been killed in a bombing raid on Eddie's birthday. Eddie clipped a poem from *Stars and Stripes* which expressed our feelings about David and all the boys who met death in France.

Tribute

I saw him wink as he sped by,
Half-hidden in a monster tank,
A lad whose cap was on his ear,
His smile his only hint of rank.

The joy of life danced in his eyes,
The fields were his and all the sky,
Though there was much he hoped to keep,
He laughed as he went out to die.

One thing I know, and know it well
And it is now my only cheer
Each spring will bloom, where'er he falls,
The gayest flowers of the year.

T/5 Peter Alfano.

After two months of continuous fighting in Normandy, the Allied casualty reports listed 16,434 dead, 76,535 wounded and 19,704 missing-in-action. The fields of Normandy would forever be crowded with "the gayest flowers of the year" and white stone markers.

CHAPTER 32

Poppy wrote from Scotland, but without leave it was impossible to schedule a rendezvous. We were lucky to get an occasional night off to frolic in Weymouth. Between April 17 and August 13, we had 58 bookings of *Stars Without Garters* at which we gave multiple performances, with only a 30-minute break to clear the theatre and get the next audience seated. After D-Day, the Luftwaffe counter-attacked with their powerful, new V-1 rocket bombs. Numerous buildings in all major cities were destroyed, and thousands died. Often our performances were interrupted by enemy raids. In Portsmouth, we went underground for an hour until the all-clear sounded. We remained in blackout, but we completed the show by a flood of light from the GIs' flashlights, just like Carole Landis and Martha Raye in *Four Jills and a Jeep*.

Finally we received 48-hour passes in mid-August. Eddie cabled Eric and we went to London. Eric hosted a spectacular cocktail party in our honor where we met Noel Coward, Peggy Ashcroft, Benjamin Britten, Terrance Rattigan, Ivor Novello, et al. Whee! We luxuriated in lots of good, inner-circle theatrical gossip. Beatrice Lillie arrived with an entourage including Cyril Ritchard, Madge Elliot, Moya Nugent and handsome, teenaged actor Grant Tyler who served as a substitute for Miss Lillie's son killed in action. Miss Lillie told us that Dame Lilian had requested our services for hospital entertainment. "I contacted Colonel Smythe. He agreed for you to appear at the opening of the Stage Door Canteen on September 20," she continued. "Bing Crosby is the headliner and, of course, yours truly. We'll have great fun!" We were thrilled.

After the party, Eric, Eddie and I scampered to Le Boeuf sur le Toit where we met Major Brutus who introduced us to "Essie," Lord Tradegar's hooty male secretary. Essie invited us to the Lord's flat for fun and games. The group included American flier Lieutenant Tom

Collier, Barry Sinclair (Ivor Novello's ex-lover), a chorus boy, a Scottish colonel and a Canadian captain. We drank lots of Pimms, and Essie taught us a new toast: "One's all right, two's the most. Three under the table, four under the host." We played "The Truth Game." Each player wrote the most personal question he could devise. The identical slips were placed in a container. Then each player drew a question and answered truthfully. The sexy, campy questions and answers were the perfect prelude to the orgy that followed. We operated at fever pitch until 0600, when the officers had to report for duty.

Lord Tradegar returned that morning. He and Essie treated us to a champagne lunch at the Ritz. The Lord was gracious and witty. They were journeying to Horsham the next day, and he invited us to travel with them.

When Eric departed for the theatre that night, he warned us, "Watch out for the Bob Hopes!"—the nickname for the V-2 rockets. "Just bob down and hope for the best." But the Jerries sent their newest flying bombs other places, and we enjoyed a quiet night at Eric's palatial Mayfair abode. At breakfast we ate wild, white raspberries sweeter that the domestic red ones. Eric said the berries came from thickets in Shakespeare's orchard, but he may have been pulling my leg.

Lord Tradegar and Essie arrived at Victoria Station with four large suitcases filled with hundreds of pounds of jade, two travel cases and a cage with Essie's pet mice. The Lord had decided to move his jade collection to his country estate. Eddie and I each grabbed a valise, and the four of us lugged the valuable cargo on the train. The Lord promptly produced a bottle of gin. We didn't have glasses or cups, so the Lord grabbed the water bowl from the mice's cage, cleaned it, and filled it with water. We took turns guzzling a slug of good gin from the bottle and chasing it with a slurp of rat-bowl water. After each turn, the drinker rushed to refill the bowl for the next one. After several turns, we developed the silly giggles and forgot about the chaser. When we reached Horsham, Eddie and I were tempted momentarily to accept the Lord's invitation to visit a few days, but sanity prevailed. We helped them unload the jade and jumped back on the train amid gales of laughter and promises to write. Within the week, Essie wrote that the Lord's Knightsbridge flat had received a direct hit. Everything was destroyed and many of their neighbors were killed.

Nobody had to tell us that the time for us to sail to the far shore was imminent. Paris was liberated, and the advance into Germany was next.

The rumor mill predicted that the war would be over by Christmas. Our platoon transferred to Blandford on detached service for a group of five hospitals. We were in the process of developing a second company show, *For Free*. We auditioned the new material on those wonderfully brave, convalescent men who had survived the invasion.

That summer thousands of German POWs were shipped to England, Canada and the United States. One afternoon, ten German prisoners were cutting weeds near our camp. The truck to haul them to the stockade didn't return at the appointed time, and the guard brought them over to wait in the shade of our barracks. One of the guys spoke English. We asked the POW, who had been captured on the Cherbourg peninsula, about France and Germany. He told us that France would be a safe place to be stationed because Germany couldn't hold out much longer. He said their army was forced to use teenage boys and women as replacements. It was difficult for us to comprehend that those amiable, handsome young Bavarian farmers were the enemy. War, we concluded, was impossible to understand.

CHAPTER 33

On September 17, the company traveled in a 19-vehicle convoy to the Weymouth docks where we boarded a LST. Due to the number of soldiers on the crossing, there was a shortage of bunks. Some of us were assigned to sailors' quarters. The sailor in the next bunk and I had a long conversation about everything under sun. Eventually he told me that some of the guys on the LST liked to fool around and asked me if any of the men in our company liked male action. I told him it suited me okay. We arranged to meet in the stern of the ship after lights out. I told him I had a buddy, and he said he'd bring a buddy, too.

Eddie and I spent the afternoon on deck and watched the ship-filled harbor and the water-taxis making deliveries. I spotted Lew Granger's ship. "Captain Nash, Eddie and I have a good friend on the Melville. Any chance for us to take a taxi over there for an hour or two?" I asked.

"I don't see why not," the Captain replied. When the next taxi pulled alongside, Eddie and I climbed down the rope ladder and went to the Melville to pay a social call. Lew gave us a grand tour of the repair ship. When we were ready to leave, there was a water-taxi jam. Our LST signaled, "Send Fuller and Carpenter back." The guys on the Melville responded, "No taxi until after chow." So we broke bread with all our torpedo-juice drinking buddies and had a gay 'ole time.

Back on the LST, passengers and crew enjoyed Bing Crosby's performance in *Going My Way* and went bananas for the tuneful "Swinging On a Star." The movie was excellent, but it was small consolation for missing the chance to appear with 'Der Bingle' and Bea Lillie at the London Stage Door Canteen opening. After lights out, Eddie and I kept our date with the two sailors. Hot fraternization deep in the bowels of the LST was large consolation indeed. Well, all reet!

The English Channel belied its ugly reputation. The water was peaceful and cornflower blue. The sun shone bright and warm. Many of us sunbathed on deck. Phil Dickinson hooted, "Some war!" We passed Cherbourg, cruised down the Normandy shore, and edged onto the sand at Utah Beach. At dawn on a dew-drenched field a few miles inland, we chopped and raked a space to accommodate company headquarters. We pitched pup tents along four imaginary streets. We dug toilet facilities, cleared an area for the kitchen and gathered firewood. We dined on C-rations, cleaned our weapons and drilled all afternoon. Two-Bar FUBAR would have loved it.

We hiked four miles into St. Germain to see a mediocre USO show. It inspired us to do something better. We gave several performances of *For Free!* on the outdoor stage at St. Germain. "Tax Payers Pay For It! 4-Fs Crave For It. We Give It To You *FOR FREE!* A Show For G.I. Joe." The crowds went wild with appreciation. The band gave several concerts and we showed movies under the stars. Our athletic personnel organized softball and volleyball competitions among the units in the bivouac area. Tent life lasted a week until orders came through to move to Post Headquarters in Le Mans.

We convoyed 160 miles through newly liberated towns and villages. Along the way, laughing children and cheering adults greeted us. We depleted our supplies of candy and gum by mid-morning, but all day we received apples from grateful Frenchmen who grabbed our hands. In heavily-blitzed Perriers, we stopped and drank cider. In beautiful Coutances, we sipped vintage wines. In Laval, two pretty laughing girls tossed fresh peaches to us from a balcony. "Les Americains!" they shouted over and over. They applauded as if we were giving a performance. We saw what freedom meant to people who had been without it for four long years.

The red brick buildings of La Caserne Chanzy, General Pershing's headquarters in the Great War, were our new home. Many battalions were based there. The Red Ball Express—famous for its daring exploits of getting petrol, ammunition and food to advancing front-line troops—operated out of the fortress. The barracks showed signs of recent occupation by the "master race," but reassuring messages from the ubiquitous Kilroy greeted us too. God bless Kilroy. That GI told us that he had gone forth to make it safe for us to follow. In less than 24 hours, we were a functioning company. We showed movies, played jam sessions and gave three performances of the company shows. In a few days, the 34th was scattered over a 50-mile radius to operate cinemas in Chartes, Dreux, Auneau and Rennes. In October our company report listed 394 film showings, 26 stage shows and 33 concerts. Eddie and I soon found a favorite watering hole in Le Mans, Madame Nini's at 13, Place de l' Eperon. We made friends with the owners, Monsieur and Madame Rachet, and their hooty barmaid, Louise.

We gave many performances on the portable stage in rain, sleet and finally, snow. Many Frenchmen sighed that it was the earliest and worst winter in memory. I was plagued by a series of minor illnesses—sore throat, fever, sniffles—but I had neither the time nor inclination to cater to them.

One particularly crowded night at Madame Nini's, I met a hot-to-trot pilot in the outdoor pissoir. He got me off, but I had a runny nose and raw throat. I couldn't reciprocate. "You wait right here," I told him. "I've got a horny buddy. You'll like him." Even under the sheltered walkway, I got drenched by icy rain. Inside it took me a full five minutes to maneuver through the throng to Eddie who stood by the front entrance. I explained the situation and off he went. Just before he reached the rear exit, the pilot entered and got lost in the crowd. I motioned to Eddie but he didn't see me. Twenty minutes later, Eddie returned. "Wow," he said, "that was some hot action, Jackson."

"What action?" I asked. "The pilot came in just a minute before you went out the door. I tried to signal you."

An astounded Eddie said, "Well, fiddle-dee fuck. I went into the head and a pilot was taking a leak. I told him, 'Hurry up. Turn around. I haven't got much time.' He did. We did. I came back."

SNAFU? FUBAR? Not at all. Different pilot, same situation. We laughed and ordered another Calvados.

CHAPTER 34

Private R. J. Sherman
Company A—368th Engineers Regiment
Somewhere in France

October 25, 1944

Dear Sergeant Carpenter and Fellow GIs,

    I'm not much on "fan mail" but I do want you boys to know that we all enjoyed your show tonight. Not only one but all of you are "On the Tit."
    On behalf of myself and eight other guys here, I wonder if you would do us a favor? We would really like a copy of the monologue "Hell" which you presented. Boy, you really put it over.
    Could you do it for us? What the "Hell"—it wouldn't take long! Hope we aren't asking for a trade secret.

Yours for more shows and thanks,
Robert Sherman

    The "Hell" monologue appeared in the "Poets Corner" section of an early issue of *Yank*. I immediately sent a copy of the poem to Private Sherman and thanked him for his kind words, and told him how much I enjoyed doing the piece.

HELL

> Just what is meant by the word called hell?
> Sometimes they say it's cold as hell, and
> Sometimes they say it's hot as hell.

> When it rains hard, it's hell they say.
> It's also hell when it's dry.
> They hate like hell to see it snow.
> It's a helluva wind when it starts to blow.
> Now how in the hell can anyone tell
> What they mean by this word called hell?
> This Army life is hell we say.
> When we get in late, it's hell to pay.
> When we start to yell it's a helluva note
> And it's hell when the detail we have to tote.
> It's hell when the doctor sends his bills
> For a helluva lot of trips and pills.
> Yet when you hear this, you know real well
> Just what they mean by this word called hell.
> Hell, yes! Hell, no!
> The hell you did; the hell you didn't.
> What the hell?
> The hell you do; the hell you don't.
> The hell it is.
> The hell with you.
> Who the hell?
> Oh, hell where?
> What the hell do you think I care?
> But the hell of it is,
> It's sure as hell we don't know
> What the hell hell is.
> Oh, hell!

I closed with an old burlesque joke made popular by comedian Red Skelton:

> Lieutenant Helen Hunt asked me to make the following announcement. She found a wallet. Anyone who lost a wallet with no ID and 200 dollars, can go to hell and hunt for it.

CHAPTER 35

Front-line troops were sent to Rennes for R & R (rest and relaxation). Our first performance for the men at Rennes was most memorable. The officers and enlisted men in the audience acted like an enormous fraternity; they had survived the invasion and months under enemy fire. We had played to appreciative audiences in the past, but these men from the front lines exploded with gratitude. Following the show, concurrent parties in our honor were staged at the Officers' Club and the Enlisted Men's Club. Members of the cast shuttled between them. The cognac and champagne flowed, and the embraces and bone-crushing handshakes never stopped.

Lieutenant Robinson tried to get our platoon organized for the return to Le Mans at midnight; however, he was ordered by several higher-ranking officers not to break up the parties. When we finally pulled into the fortress at five the next morning, Captain Nash was understandably charged up. Lieutenant Robinson caught hell and the entire platoon was restricted to barracks for 48 hours.

General Patton issued requests for infantry-trained soldiers to join the Third Army as replacements. Captain Nash, provoked by the Rennes situation, decided to transfer Eddie, John Bucklin and me.

Two-Bar FUBAR's stool pigeons had reported that we were "queers" and ruining the reputation of the company. Lieutenants Bernstein and Bawn pressured Captain Nash, who became self-conscious since many times he had been accused of being a homosexual due to his somewhat prissy manner.

We went to the post infirmary for a medical okay before we shipped out. The doctors discovered that Eddie had a slight heart murmur. They turned him down. As a sergeant, I was considered a special prize for

Patton. I asked the doctor whether my allergy to wool made any difference. He replied, "Good God, yes. But I will need to see your medical confirmation." I rushed to the barracks and checked through my stuff. I could not find the letter that I had carried since my days at Pine Camp. I went to Captain Nash, who had seen the letter, and I told him of its mysterious disappearance. I asked whether he would verify its existence. Since Captain Nash was a dear and honest man, he honored my request. Once again, Eddie and I managed to avoid separation by the skin of our teeth. Johnny Bucklin passed the medical exam and shipped out that same afternoon.

After chow I went to Captain Nash. I requested a private meeting with him and anyone else who had knowledge of the rumors. Thirty minutes later, we were seated in the Captain's office facing Top Sergeant Leon Temple, Sergeant Alger Mason, Private Teddy Chapman and the Captain. I asked who had proof that Eddie and I were "queers." No one would supply a name. I then stated that I was hurt that we had not been consulted about the rumors prior to the attempts to get rid of us. Eddie spoke up and said that on numerous occasions he had been forced to publicly deny that Captain Nash was a homosexual, which he had done in the presence of everyone in the room except the Captain. It was embarrassing, but Eddie had no choice. Unless positive proof existed, we did not expect to be harassed or punished in the future because someone in the company did not like us. Yes, we were gay, but admission was not an option. It would have destroyed our military careers. Captain Nash said that he was sorry about the situation and that he was relieved not to lose us as valuable members of the company.

After the meeting, Eddie and I returned to the barracks. The entire show platoon was frozen in fear that they had lost us. I laughed and said, "We're not going anywhere without all of you if I can help it." They gave us hugs of approval and shed happy tears. We felt so honored. We told the men exactly what had happened. They wanted to find out who the trouble-makers were and "beat the living shit out of them." We never discovered the identify of the bigots who created the problems. We were not cowards. We wanted to stay with the 34th Special Service Company. The work suited us and we wanted to stay together. Due to poor vision, Bucklin was rejected for front-line duty, and he returned to our company about four weeks later.

On election day, November 6, we were proud that the United States was the only major country which held a national election during wartime. We charted the election results on a big map in company headquarters. It was a close race, but the men and women in uniform overseas swung the election because we realized that no other man in government could handle the rigors of foreign wars like President Roosevelt. He was re-elected for an unprecedented fourth term. Hurrah!

CHAPTER 36

On November 9, the show platoon went on detached service to Soissons, 40 miles south of the Belgian border. We passed through Paris, but our orders would not permit us to stop. We spent the first two days in Soissons repairing and cleaning the entertainment center. At least the Rec Hall had a decent stage. Even though the place was a shambles, the projectionists showed movies the night we arrived.

During the night, the Supply Company of the 82nd Airborne Division arrived from Holland with the duffel bags of the paratroopers. On our way to breakfast the next morning, we passed an enormous drill field with hundreds of duffel bags neatly arranged in long rows. That night after chow about a third of the bags had been picked up. Eddie said, "Well, I guess the rest of the men will be here by reveille and we'll need to be ready to 'trod the boards' by evening."

The next morning, there were gaps in the longs rows of bags, but over 50 percent had not been claimed. Eddie and I looked at each other in horror as we realized that the owners of the remaining bags would not be coming back. After breakfast we got the official word that both the 82nd and the 101st Airborne Divisions had suffered heavy casualties in the bridge jumps at Nijmegen, Holland. General James Gavin paid us a visit at the Rec Hall to find out when we would be ready to present a live show. "Sir," I answered, "when you and the men are ready, we're ready."

"Good, Sergeant. Tonight then," he responded. After the performance, General Gavin came backstage. He shook my hand. "Sergeant, *Stars Without Garters* is the best soldier show I have ever seen," he said. "I want you and the platoon to join me and my men at the Service Club for beers when you finish up here."

"Yes, sir. Thank you, sir," I replied. General Gavin's men called him "Gentleman Jim." We understood the nickname after we observed him interacting with them. The guys could talk to him about anything, and he listened.

One afternoon hundreds of paratroopers watched a lone plane circling an open field. When I asked what was happening, the men told me that "Gentleman Jim" was testing a new parachute, which he did each time a shipment arrived. The crowd gazed in silence when he jumped. When he landed safely, all the men cheered. I whistled and clapped louder than anyone. I loved "Gentleman Jim."

After we gave a dozen performances, we moved to Suippes to entertain General Maxwell Taylor's 101st Paratroopers, the Screaming Eagles. General Taylor had been called back to the States for emergency meetings and General Anthony McAuliffe, second-in-command, was in charge. General McAuliffe personally greeted us when we arrived. He was charming, handsome and rugged. Following our first performance, he came backstage and told us that our show was just what his men needed and that he would always fondly remember our revue and classy presentation. Now, I had two hero-defenders.

We gave three performances of both shows in Suippes. After our final performance, Howard Baymiller—a hooty, hyper saxophonist—rushed backstage and impishly announced, "'Ole Two-Bar FUBAR was in the audience and he's on his way backstage right now."

"Well," I said, "he finally saw the show. I hope he liked what he's been missing." Within minutes I was facing Major Fletcher. I saluted.

Between puffs on his cigarette, he said, "Sergeant Carpenter, good show. I'm proud of my old company. It was a fine production."

It was the first time I had ever heard him pay anyone a compliment. "Thanks, Captain," I said, "I mean Major." He seemed embarrassed and continued to puff away. I broke the silence. "Major Fletcher, you're smoking. I remember you used to tell us it was a nasty habit and a waste of time. Why did you change your mind?"

He stared at me and appeared deep in thought. After a lengthy pause he said, "Hunger. I've been in dangerous territory without the usual breaks for chow, and hunger was a constant companion." He then moved on and spoke with all the cast. He seemed genuinely interested in his former company. Each of us showed respect for the uniform he wore, but I doubt if any member of the cast felt true regard for the uptight, unhappy man. We just felt sorry for the men who were currently under his command.

Troops were stationed all around Reims, touted as the Champagne

Center of the World. Each time we passed the Piper Heidsik warehouse, we purchased large bottles of champagne for less than a dollar. Usually each man bought two or more bottles to drink on the return to camp. None of our guys ever drank before a performance, but after the show we guzzled champagne as if it were soda pop. We enjoyed many happy hours on the long rides back to the base. All of the cafes in the area were packed with GIs. Sex with women or men was readily available in the small towns on the streets and in the pissoirs. It was easy to make out, and no one paid much attention to who was doing what with whom. We wanted to stop and carouse with them but we had to meet our curfew.

We spent every morning engaged in calisthenics, close-order drill and weapons maintenance. In the afternoons, we showed films, rehearsed, or distributed books and equipment. On the few evenings we did not give performances, Eddie and I played bridge or shot the bull at the Service Club where "Gentleman Jim" usually stopped in to chat. The paratroopers were friendly and treated us like celebrities.

We were chewing the fat at the Service Club with Big Red—a sergeant who had jumped in Italy, France and Holland—when he told us that he was going to meet some buddies at a nearby brothel. He asked us to join him. Eddie had an assignment to run a film, so he couldn't accept Big Red's invitation to join the pussy brigade. I tried to beg off because I was supposed to meet a buddy, Dan Furlong, for a card game at 8:30 p.m. "Hell, Ty," Big Red said, "we can knock off a fast piece and be back by then."

The next thing I knew, Big Red and I were hoofing down a muddy, country road to the whorehouse. I didn't have the courage to tell Red that I wasn't interested and why. He had a bottle of cognac, and we took several belts as we walked. Red told me about his many jumps, hand-to-hand combat and buddies killed in action. He related that once during battle, General Gavin had crawled to his foxhole to make sure that he was okay. Red was so proud that the General knew him by name. "Shit, I'd follow 'Gentleman Jim' anywhere, even down the barrel of a cannon if he asked me to."

The whorehouse was an old dance hall. Benches lined each wall of the enormous room. Several hundred guys were ahead of us and there were only five girls to accommodate the horde. All of the men were swigging booze and telling jokes. I felt safe because I could use drunkenness as an excuse to leave in a couple of hours. My feeling of protection lasted a full five minutes standing at the end of the line. Big Red was known by many of the men, but I was recognized by all of them. The four paratroopers ahead of us jumped up. "Sergeant Carpenter, let me shake your hand. Good show."

"Here's Ty to give 'em Hell!"

"Man, I just threw my third fuck; you take my place."

"I'm not special, guys," I said, 'I'll wait for my turn."

"You're not gonna wait while I'm on this line," Red said.

Then the line crumbled to acknowledge preferential treatment for me. I was slapped on the back, given many swigs from many bottles and passed around the entire room. In less than 30 minutes, I found myself on the left side of the entrance at the head of the line. I looked across at Big Red on the right side of the door still near the end of the line. Oh, God! How I wanted to trade places with him.

A short, dumpy, frizzy blonde in a chemise released her trick with one hand and grabbed me with the other. She led me to a second-floor room with a single bed. I tried to tell her no, but she spoke no English and I spoke no French. She shed her chemise and flopped on the bed. I undressed. I put a rubber on my flaccid cock and climbed on. After several attempts at penetration, she grabbed my cock, jerked the condom off, and went down on me. I closed my eyes and conjured up mental pictures of the well-endowed sailor on the LST. She finished me off in no time. She hopped up and donned her chemise. I was wrong. She knew enough English to say, "two dollars," and she pointed to a small dish on the dresser. She left. I dressed and rushed down to the ballroom. I passed the blonde and her next trick on the stairs. Big Red had barely moved in the line. I took a big gulp from his brandy bottle. He wanted me to stay around for an encore.

"No, buddy. Once is enough for me."

Eddie and Danny Furlong waited for me at the Service Club. I apologized for being late and tried to joke about my trek to the brothel with Big Red. Eddie appreciated that I had experienced another milestone and even saw some humor in the situation. Danny, a straight buddy I met at Mass, accepted the episode as perfectly natural. He howled when I related a slightly edited version of the events.

CHAPTER 37

On December 12 the Airborne Divisions were put on full-war alert. Something big was happening. Our orders were to show films around the clock. Thank God, headquarters kept us well supplied with new movies. For two days, I ran three escapist musicals which the fellows liked: *Here Come The Waves* with Betty Hutton and Bing Crosby warbling "Accentuate The Positive"; the all-star *Hollywood Canteen* with Bette Davis and our dancing friend, Joan McCracken; and *Music For Millions* with Marsha Hunt and June Allyson. On December 15, the motor pool feverishly placed all vehicles in convoys, and the paratroopers departed. We expected orders to follow them, but no word came. By reveille the camp was as inactive as it had been the day we arrived. We went to chow with a skeleton crew. We learned that the Germans were making a major offensive in the Ardennes. "The Battle of the Bulge" had commenced.

After 36 hours of anxious waiting, we received orders to return to Le Mans. As we approached Paris, I reckoned it might be our only chance to see the world's most romantic city. Before I could develop a scheme, providence lent a hand. Our weapons carrier needed ball bearings replaced. The breakdown gave us a perfect excuse for a three-hour tour of Paris. We invaded the city in small groups. Eddie, Alger Mason, Johnny Romano and I started off at the railway station, where cleaning women mopped around our feet while we pissed. Next we stopped in a cafe for Calvados to fortify ourselves against the cold, penetrating drizzle and contrasting purplish mists that enveloped the city. Many prostitutes stood near the entrances to the Red Cross Building on the Boulevard Capucines and tried to entice us. The citizens of Paris were in a near state of panic over the German assault in Belgium. Men and women cried and waved their hands frantically when they discussed the events. We dashed through the streets like demons and managed to take pictures of each other in front of the Arc de Triomphe and the Eiffel Tower.

Despite our finally realized tour of Paris, neither Eddie nor I felt very gay when we departed. Eddie said, "Well, baby, I guess General Bradley figured us 'ball-bearing WACs' wouldn't be much help in Belgium." I laughed. Eddie's clever declaration temporarily relieved our apprehension about the major battles in progress north of the French border. I sang "Swinging On a Star," and Eddie joined in. We masked our dread with song.

High anxiety reigned at the fortress in Le Mans. The Allied air forces were grounded by fog and mist for the first seven days of the battle, but on December 23 the skies cleared, allowing deployment of Allied planes. The German advance was halted, but the battle raged on as the enemy produced endless supplies of fresh troops and powerful new tanks.

It wasn't a merry holiday season. We ran films and performed live shows for the troops in transit. Captain Nash called us together on Christmas Eve. We listened to President Roosevelt's Christmas address on the radio. The Captain read us a commendatory letter from Brigadier-General Solbert, Chief of Special Services in the ETO: "...I congratulate the entire company on their accomplishments. You have met and overcome many problems of operation and have grown in importance as a valuable service contributing to the success of our combat troops." The commendation was a good gift, but MGM gave us the best gift, the wonderful *Meet Me In St. Louis*. When Judy Garland sang "Have Yourself a Merry Little Christmas" to moppet Margaret O'Brien, all the men in the company melted. That song and film expressed everything that we prayed for.

We received a letter from Kimo Dennis with a picture of him taken on a palm-covered island. He wrote that crucial fighting abounded on that front, too. On Christmas Day, Eddie and I ate two holiday dinners. The first was supplied by the army and the second was provided by our friends Monsieur and Madame Rachet, the owners of Madame Nini's. On that bleak, snowy Monday, *Stars and Stripes* reported that Major Glenn Miller, conductor of the Army Air Corps Band and popular Big Band leader, had been missing since December 15. His plane disappeared over the English Channel. No members of the band were with him. Two days after Christmas, enemy aircraft bombed Paris. The raid was brief and caused minimal damage and few casualties; however, it was one more indication that victory was further away than any of us wished.

Bucklin, Eddie and I were on detached service in Chartres on New Year's Eve. It was miserably cold and we couldn't find a drink for love or money to toast the New Year, so we drank coffee and ate the last of my Auntie Estelle's fruitcake, which we had liberally laced with brandy. We were thankful that we were more fortunate than most of the men in uniform that night. We were dry. We were warm. We had each other.

CHAPTER 38

During the first five weeks of 1945, the Allied Armies mounted an offensive which drove the Germans out of Belgium. We traveled all over northern France and entertained the combat-weary troops from the front lines and the replacements in transit. We gave live shows and ran films day and night. In Rennes, Corky Mainer—a young private I had hooked up with back at Gladys Mahoney's in Weymouth—came backstage after the performance.

"What's the action, Jackson?" I asked.

"Oh, I've been enjoying the wonderful winter sports up in beautiful Bastogne," he laughingly replied.

"Seriously, how was it?"

"We earned the nickname 'the Battered Bastards of Bastogne.' D-Day by comparison was almost a picnic," he said, "and I know 'cause I was there." He paused. "The Goddamn snow and ice didn't seem to bother the German sons-of-bitches. They dropped fucking leaflets offering hot chow and safety just 100 yards away if we'd surrender. And get this. The freaking mother-fuckers broadcast the song 'I Surrender Dear' over speakers. Poor dumb bastards didn't realize that shit just made us more determined. When they demanded surrender, McAuliffe issued a one-word response, 'NUTS!!!' McAuliffe was magnificent. And when the British fly-boys finally arrived with the bombs two days after Christmas, damn, talk about happy. Man, I'm here to tell you that a list of the heroes in this war will be fatter than the New York telephone directory." Corky paused. I put my arm around his shoulder and gave him a hug. "Can you get away for a few minutes?" he asked. "I've got a bottle of brandy." I found Eddie packing up for our return and I told him the situation.

"Go," Eddie said, 'I'll cover for you, but don't make it longer than 30 minutes."

I followed Corky to an empty building behind the Rec Hall. We drank and kissed. The sex was incidental. He craved affection. He hugged me close over and over, and I reciprocated. He gave me his home address. "If anything happens to me," he said, "will you write my mom and sister and tell them that I was a good soldier?"

"Sure, buddy. Anything," I said. "But kid, you'll make it. After what you've been through, you're invincible."

Both armies paid an astronomical price for the mighty battle in Belgium. Allied losses numbered almost 81,000 men. About 77,000 of the casualties were Americans. More than 100,000 Germans were killed.

The Russian army advanced slowly through Poland on the eastern front amid heavy fighting and enormous casualties. The Allied advances on the western border were also slow and bloody. Before they yielded any town or hamlet, the tenacious Jerries staged stubborn campaigns. And the daily snows hindered our advances and their retreats.

Stars and Stripes, on February 8, ran a rave review of *Stars Without Garters*. It doubly pleased us because it was not a publicity release, but an honest-to-goodness unsolicited review. The army daily had published publicity items about our company show on several occasions, such as the time we played in blackout by the GIs' flashlights, but this article really sang our praises. We were proud beyond description.

Captain Nash received an emergency request for us to fill in for a snowbound Special Service Company to the north of us, since we had access to Alsace-Lorraine. After a hazardous trek over ice-covered roads, we managed to get through. Our theatre was an unheated hangar. Thirty-five hundred troops filed in and sat on the floor. The temperature was near zero outside, but audience excitement and body heat spurred us to give a good performance of *For Free*. The men went wild over "Long-John Jenny."

> An Alsace maiden in a small cafe
> keeps the boys happy in the cutest way.
> She entertains them with a strip routine
> that's a bit naughty but not at all obscene.
> The gal in question has a brand new pair
> of Government Issue underwear.
> So as not to risk pneumonia in the early dawn,
> she does all her stripping with her long johns on.
> Her name is Jenny and she's quite a chick.
> To watch her stripping gives a solid kick.

> The band starts playing and she goes to town
> while the boys all shout, "Jenny, let your drop-seat down!"
> First she disposes of a laced silk bra
> while the Yanks all holler, "Yee Hee, Hurrah!"
> The Tommies give out with a brisk "Hip, Hip!"
> as Jenny saucily lays down her slip.
> She kicks a shoe up to the balcony
> completely exposing a shapely knee.
> Off come her stockings, one at a time,
> then she tosses her garters in the GIs' wine.
> Jenny stands lovely in her underwear,
> completely undaunted and without a care.
> You ought to hear 'em whistle when she does a bump,
> that fascinating lady with the air-cooled rump.
> Long-John Jenny is the toast of France,
> knocking 'em dead with her ventilated pants.
> Customers flock from all over the map,
> just to see Jenny let her drop-seat flap!

After the performance, 1st Lieutenant Buck Smith introduced himself. He was on detached service and had been ordered by his commanding officer to check us out. He asked me if I wrote "Long-John Jenny." I told him no, but that it was written by a soldier. Lieutenant Smith kept paying me such extravagant compliments that I began to feel embarrassed. "Listen, sir," I said, "I can't take all the credit for the show. You need to meet my co-director and our primary writer."

"Okay, Sergeant, but call me Buck," he said.

The men were striking the set and packing up. I yelled, "Fuller, take a break." Eddie joined us. "I'm Ty and this is Eddie, my closest friend."

After a few minutes of shooting the bull, Buck told us that he had gone to an auction near Paris and bought an old hearse which he converted into a bedroom on wheels. I began to get solid vibes from the stocky, handsome blonde. I asked him if we could see his hearse. "Come on," he said. I yelled to Sergeant Temple to take over for 45 minutes while we went with the Lieutenant to check on his transportation. Buck's love machine was hidden by a snow bank. Inside were two unzipped sleeping bags spread out like a double bed. He even had a storm lamp behind the bolted door so that we could see what we were doing and to whom. It was instant love.

After that, whenever Buck was nearby, we rendezvoused for an affair in his hearse. Buck had a wife and child back in the States but he preferred to cheat with men instead of women. There were many GIs like Buck—married soldiers who sought sex with other soldiers rather than the available whores.

Danny Furlong wrote in late February from a London hospital where he received treatment for bullet wounds, his souvenirs of Bastogne. For him the war was over. He expected to be shipped any day to a V.A. Hospital in Seattle near his home. He wanted me to know that he was okay and told me not to worry, but I did. I worried for him, Eddie, my brothers, myself and all the men and women in uniform.

Several days later, we received a letter from Derby.

> Miss Derby Rogers
> Prince George Hotel
> 14 East 28th Street
> New York, New York

January 2, 1945

Dearest Tyler and Eddie,

I am so sorry to be the one to tell you but Helen Luca asked me to. Poppy was killed in action the day before Thanksgiving. His plane was shot down over Mannheim, Germany. There were no survivors.

Mr. and Mrs. LaPolla received the War Department telegram the day after Christmas. Poor, sweet Helen went half crazy with grief. Moo, Pussy and I went to Bayonne to offer the little comfort we could to her and Poppy's parents. They will never get over it. Poppy was the brightest and the best. All the world will miss his genius but I think we will miss his smile the most.

Minelda came for drinks yesterday and we had a good cry. I know you are heartbroken.

Please watch out for each other and keep safe. I will write again soon.

Love,
Derby

CHAPTER 39

Mrs. Roosevelt sent the free world a valentine in her February 14 column when she announced the April planning session in San Francisco for the United Nations. Also, the first lady provided us with specifics about the conference of the Big Three—Churchill, Stalin and Roosevelt—at Yalta.

General McAuliffe was appointed commander of the 103rd Infantry Division. He requested that the 34th Special Service Company be assigned to his division. We joined the 103rd in Nancy, France. As part of the Seventh Army, we began the arduous advance toward Germany. We were the rear echelon combat troops responsible for entertainment when the front-line soldiers rotated. We crept along behind miles of big guns, tanks, trucks and jeeps. Wrecked vehicles blocked the roads so we stopped, moved, and stopped again while they were towed. And we waited for the front line to move deeper into enemy territory. We watched despondent Frenchmen attempt to repair their shattered homes with boards and sacks to keep out the snow and sleet. Many houses were beyond repair and the residents sought refuge in their barns. Cattle stood in ice-crusted pastures littered with the artifacts of combat. Two or three times a day, we saw hundreds of Allied bombers headed toward Berlin. We prayed for them. We lost track of what day it was because every day was the same, and we were never sure where we were because all the road signs had been torn down and tossed in the ditches. The sector at the front changed hands on an hourly basis; sometimes the Krauts retreated faster than we advanced. The fighting went on day and night.

After Saarbrucken, Bitche and Annweiler were taken, Seventh Army units attacked Neustadt, Neunkirchen, Kaiserslautern and Homburg. When those locations were freed, we began to cross the Rhine between Worms and Mannheim during the last week of March or the first week in April. The constant din of gunfire and exploding bombs made us edgy, but the infrequent periods of silence were even worse. We were scared all the time.

The frantic struggle to avoid death became each man's obsession. We were on constant alert for snipers and mines. Correspondent Ernie Pyle wrote just prior to his death by sniper fire, "You begin to feel that you can't go on forever without being hurt. I feel that I have used up all my chances. And I hate it. I don't want to be killed." Vehicles transporting the dead and wounded sped past headed in the opposite direction while we inched eastward. We commandeered whole villages and towns for shelter. Many of the residents had long since evacuated, because wherever we were, the fighting had been heavy just hours before. We hated being dirty, wet and cold all the time. After a while, we stopped thinking about being under fire. It was a way to avoid apprehension and fear. Paul Fussell explained, "For us there would be no way out until the war ended but sickness, wounds, or oblivion. And the war would end only as we pressed our painful daily advance. Getting it over was our sole motive."

Every few days, the fuel and ammunition supply trucks brought us new batches of films and mail. We ran films in any available space. The guys loved Joan Blondell and little Peggy Ann Garner in *A Tree Grows in Brooklyn*. The frivolous antics of Gail Russell and Diana Lynn in *Our Hearts Were Young and Gay* delighted the battle-weary GIs. We liked seeing Veronica Lake and Sonny Tufts—Eddie's co-star on Broadway in *Sing For Your Supper*—in the silly, technicolor musical, *Bring On The Girls*. Her eye was blue. When we found a theatre or church intact, we gave live shows and concerts. It was a gruesome time; laughter and music were more important than ever.

A letter from Leonard Kane, written on January 30, finally caught up with us. Lenny, who danced so brilliantly in several shows at Pine Camp, wrote that the combination of trench foot and frostbite, souvenirs of Bastogne, had forever robbed him of his talent. "...Dancing was my key to happiness. Being famous, having scads of money and all the rest never particularly appealed to me. It was just that dancing made me tremendously happy and I loved it.... We can only pray that this stupid madness will soon end."

The Allies finally drove the enemy deep into the "fatherland," but all of us were too exhausted to express strong emotion. We simply heaved sighs of gratitude that we were nearer our objective.

CHAPTER 40

Once we'd crossed the Rhine, our advance gained momentum. Mannheim was a maze of broken bricks, chunks of concrete and twisted frames of shattered buildings. Several miles beyond the bomb-wrecked city, someone in the back of the truck shouted, "Where's Mannheim?"

"We just passed it," Eddie yelled out the window. He turned to me and said, "Some of 'the gayest flowers of the year' will bloom there for Poppy."

The weather was a cruel clown. One decent day was followed by three inclement ones. Whenever we took the tops off the vehicles so that the guys could see where they were going, sleet and snow besieged us. Occasional hints of spring occurred, but the thawed roads hampered movement.

Heidelberg was the only German town we saw which would not have to be completely rebuilt. The beautiful old city—without a vestige of war—looked liked a picture postcard. The civilians waved vigorously. They were glad to see us. On the road to Stuttgart, we met many units of enemy troops—old men, boys and women—completely demoralized. They asked for food and waited to be taken prisoner. We drove on.

When we reached Ulm on Friday, April 13, we received the most shocking news since Pearl Harbor. President Roosevelt had died from a cerebral hemorrhage the previous day. His stewardship of the nation in peace and war had shown us the way to liberty for all our tomorrows. "The only thing we have to fear is fear itself.... The only way to have a friend is to be one." I cried. Eddie cried. Every man in our company cried. We loved him that much.

The road to Munich was clogged with thousands of dirty, malnourished men and women trudging westward. Many were liberated French slave-workers making their way home from the underground rocket factories where they had toiled for five years. Our convoy slowed for 20 miles, and we distributed C-rations and other food to the pitiful refugees.

We received orders to present a live show for the prison camps at Dachau. Dachau had been liberated by the front echelon two days before. We thought we were slated to give a show for a few hundred Allied POWs. We were totally unprepared for the atrocities of the Holocaust!

Each barracks held several hundred living skeletons. Many were clad only in skimpy rags that covered their privates. The dirt floors were deep with excrement, urine and vomit. Long, wide planks had been placed over parts of the area. Sick, emaciated, bare-footed inmates squatted on the planks to avoid the filth. Many were so sick that they wallowed in the mire. Some of the dehumanized unfortunates relieved their diarrhea-infested bowels as we walked among them. We passed stacks of decomposing corpses destined for the ovens. Some of us wept. Some of us threw up. All of us were shaken. We marveled that anyone had survived.

We set up our portable stage. Eddie and I quickly devised a musical program. Several thousand of the poor wretches huddled on the ground as close to the stage as they could get. Thank God, it was a warm, sunny day. I emceed with the aid of an interpreter. We performed every upbeat song in our repertoire. The audience literally rescued our sanity with approving cheers. The joyous smiles and laughter which flowed from that sea of broken humanity were surely the most rewarding response any group of performers had ever received. After the finale, I asked for audience requests. A great clamor of "Teegerrieg! Teegerrieg! Teegerrieg!" poured forth. I didn't understand, but the fellows in the band caught on and went right into "Tiger Rag," and the audience responded with the tiger's roar. If we hadn't always understood or appreciated the significance of the war before, we did now.

Corky Mainer approached me while we were packing up. He gave me a monumental hug. He told us that the situation was mild compared to what it had been when his unit arrived two days before. He described the bloody massacre of German guards shot by Allied soldiers and liberated inmates unable to contain their rage. "Will we ever be able to forget this?" he asked. I shook my head and sighed.

That afternoon we met up with the advancing Russian army in the small town of Weilheim. After we organized our assigned quarters and had chow, Bucklin and I went out on pass. The streets were crowded with jubilant Russian and American soldiers. The GIs were intrigued by the Russian female soldiers. Everyone partied up and down the streets as if the war were over.

Johnny worked for an oil company in the Middle East before the war. He had made several trips to Russia. He explained that the Russians were a very friendly people. "Greet them with laughter and say Russki, Russki," he said. "Usually they will hug you and kiss you, both men and women."

I followed John's lead when we encountered three handsome soldiers. "Russki, Russki, ahh!" They spoke enough English to tell us that stacks of German cameras had been confiscated and dumped in the town square for Allied soldiers. We followed them. They met a buddy who told them about wine cellars in wealthy homes on the outskirts of town. We forgot about cameras and went in search of hootch.

We found an unoccupied mansion and located the basement entrance. A Russian boy smashed the door in. We went deep into the bowels of the cellar. Icicles clung to the rock walls. We hit the jackpot. The racks were laden with hundreds of bottles. Johnny and I drank and cavorted with the Russians all over that elegant house until an hour before curfew. We kissed the Russians a fond farewell and then stuffed our jackets with as many bottles as we could carry.

When we reached the entrance to headquarters, neither Johnny nor I remembered the password. MPs passed and we hid in some heavy shrubbery until they were out of sight. An iron-rail fence surrounded our barracks. I placed my clanking loot on the ground and scaled the fence. Bucklin passed all the booze through the fence and climbed over. We thought we were home free, but our company guard challenged our noisy approach. "Who goes there?"

I yelled out, "Shit, if you don't know me by now, you'll just have to shoot me. I forgot the fucking password." He let us go, but we still had to sign in. Outside the entrance to the company office, I stumbled and one of the many bottles inside my jacket slipped and crashed on the pavement. Captain Nash opened the door and saw us trying to clean up the glass fragments. He just glared at us. I broke the silence. "I'm sorry, Captain Nash, sir. I just dropped the present I had for you."

Johnny hastily offered, "I have an extra one for the Captain." Still the Captain did not speak. We signed in and saluted. When we staggered into the barracks, the guys greeted us with the news of Hitler's suicide. "Hubba, hubba!" someone shouted. We broke open several bottles for a toast.

We traveled to Garmisch-Partenkirchen the following day. When we passed Oberamergau, home of the famous *Passion Play*, Eddie said, "When the war's over, we'll come back to see the play. It'll help to erase the memory of the terrible things we saw at Dachau." The first thing posted on the company bulletin board at Garmisch headquarters was an order restricting Bucklin and me to house arrest for the next week. Fraternization with hot Russians and lots of booze more than compensated for a few missed passes.

We slowly made our way to Austria. Frequent snowfalls on the winding mountain roads increased our appreciation for the signs of spring on the banks of beautiful aquamarine lakes and rivers in the valleys. Each afternoon we entertained thousands of troops billeted in the mountain villages. On May 7 we reached Innsbruck. General McAuliffe and the brass occupied the lovely chalets which dotted the mountainside. We were billeted in comfortable, three-story apartment houses near the Innsbruck Opera House, a scaled-down version of the great Vienna Opera House which had perfect acoustics and was ideal for our intimate musicals.

After we unloaded, Captain Nash announced Germany's unconditional surrender at 0241 (ETO time). Tuesday, May 8 had been declared V-E Day. We yelled, laughed and shed tears of joy. It was wonderful.

CHAPTER 41

Everyone in our V-E Day audiences was happily delirious. The spectators went wild and sang along with the actors.

I was sergeant-of-the-guard that night. My corporal-of-the-guard and I canvassed the immediate area. We discovered vacant homes in an affluent residential area. We robbed several houses looking for liquor. We didn't find booze, but we did pilfer silver, tea services, linens and fur coats. We slyly returned the ill-gotten gains to the barracks for safekeeping until we could mail the loot to the States. Yugoslavian, Czechoslovakian and Polish freedom fighters—saboteurs of the Nazi war machine in the mountains of Bavaria and Austria—were in Innsbruck for the celebration. When we met a group of freedom fighters who recognized us from the show, they told us, by using a combination of fractured English and body language, that the Nazi army's liquor supply was stashed in the basement of the Innsbruck Hospital, guarded by a German colonel and other Nazi officers in charge of prisoners. I took advantage of being a sergeant with a rifle. Two cast members and I went to the hospital. I demanded to see the officer in charge. The orderlies, like frightened robots, fetched the Colonel. I demanded access to the wines. The Nazi Colonel saluted and led us to the supply. We filled the three duffel bags we had brought to haul our booty. We saluted and left.

Thirty minutes after our haul, Allied officers arrived at the hospital and installed no-trespassing signs on the main gate. They confiscated the remaining booze for the brass. We had just barely made it, but we got more than our share. We were the company heroes because we provided the Victory punch! Hubba, hubba!

Twice I was assigned guard duty at the hospital, the holding area for captured SS troops. Once, the Nazi Colonel—whom I had bullied into showing us where the liquor was stored—acknowledged me with a short nod and interesting eye contact. He was certainly a gay brother or else he would have reported me.

We gave a minimum of three performances a day at the Opera House. Trucks transported several thousand Russian, English and American servicemen from the surrounding areas to the theatre each day. We had great fun with the freedom fighters. They loved our shows and were much impressed by what they perceived as our celebrity status. We were the first Americans that they had ever met, and they were fascinated. We were equally fascinated by those rugged, brave men in tattered, makeshift uniforms. We communicated with some of them when we could in the universal language of slap and tickle.

After Germany capitulated, we had lots of free time. Peter Serino, General McAuliffe's master sergeant, became our good friend when we were stationed in Suippes before the Battle of the Bulge. Peter orchestrated our transfer to the 103rd Infantry Division. He hosted unbelievable parties in his chalet for gays of all ranks. It was great fun to mingle with the brass on the mountain when we were on pass.

One night Peter told his gay guests about an unscheduled inspection by officers from Ike's headquarters. McAuliffe was out when the delegation arrived. One of the secretaries—a soldier nicknamed "Rita" who always wore a hint of make-up—greeted the visiting dignitaries and explained that the General would be right back. "She" then returned to "her" desk, picked up "her" compact and touched up "her" nose. Not very subtle, but "Rita" made a point. When McAuliffe returned, the monitors conferred with him but did not mention "Rita." Afterwards they retired to the General's chalet for cocktails. One of the visitors commented, "General McAuliffe, you have a most unusual office staff."

"I'm not sure I understand what you mean," the General replied.

"They seemed a little different from the usual GIs," the guest insisted.

"You must be referring to the feminine characteristics exhibited by some of the men," the General stated. "Well, for the most part I have a very efficient staff. If I could exchange some of the more masculine types for other feminine ones, I would have the best run office in the ETO." The General's unexpected response quelled the monitor's query.

When Peter told the story, he did delightful impressions of the people. We laughed like hyenas, but actually we were quite proud that our gay brothers were recognized as outstanding workers. Peter was a giddy goose at parties, but at work he was a professional soldier. He was even tough when necessary. All the men in the division liked and respected Peter.

Marlene Dietrich brought her show to Innsbruck. She stayed at General McAuliffe's chalet. Peter introduced us. It was a thrill to hobnob with the enchanting, gregarious film star. We saw her show and she saw ours. She performed at the Opera House for a week. While she was there, our platoon went on detached service to perform for men stationed in the mountains too far to be conveniently transported. We gave three performances a day. On the second night of the mountain tour, we were delightfully surprised when Stephen, Eddie's bartender buddy at the Dizzy Club, came backstage. Age and the rigors of army life had enhanced Stephen's natural good looks. At 30, he was more beautiful than Tyrone Power. We chatted about mutual gay friends in uniform scattered all over the globe.

"I've been going crazy," Stephen told us. "I've been so lonesome for a close buddy." His breathing became uneven. "I had a friend in North Africa, but we were separated at the invasion of Sicily. He died at Salerno." He held his breath as tears flowed. "I loved him very much." Eddie placed an arm around Stephen's shoulder. "Christ, it's good to know that you guys had the good luck to stay together," Stephen continued. "I'm happy for you and envious at the same time." We visited all night with him and his company of Mountain Rangers. It was a wonderful reunion. On our return to Innsbruck, Captain Nash gave us the official word that our company would return to the States in a matter of days. We gave many exciting farewell performances at the Opera House.

Our final days in Austria were one long continuous party. We still had plenty of liquor from the hospital raid. Every night there were mad, wild marvelous gay and straight parties in the chalets on the mountain. On Eddie's 34th birthday, we took the lift to a fabulous party at Peter's chalet. On the return trip, I struck up a conversation with a sexy paratrooper on his return from the Red Cross Club, which was housed in the mountain-top ski lodge. He recognized us from our stage appearances. We strolled with Lucky Foster through the deserted streets until we found an isolated grove of evergreens. We drank cherry schnapps and swapped war experiences. Eventually we engaged in a menage à trois there in the woods on a soft pallet of pine needles.

On the hike back to base at dawn, the sweet, innocent soldier said to Eddie, "This isn't catching is it?"

"No, Lucky," Eddie replied in a Virginia O'Brien deadpan. "And contrary to public opinion, it's not the way Kay Francis got her start in show business." Lucky laughed. He gave us a wallet photo of himself and told us that if we ever got to Greenville, South Carolina to look him up.

On our last night in Austria, Eddie and I had film assignments to show *Gaslight* which starred Ingrid Bergman and Joseph Cotten, Eddie's radio co-star on the Mercury Theatre. We were so impressed by the performance of the young actress who played the querulous maid. We predicted a big future for Angela Lansbury.

CHAPTER 42

We left at 3:00 a.m. on June 9, 1945 and convoyed northwest for 12 hours to Schwaebisch Gmuend, Germany, near Stuttgart. We occupied an entire neighborhood for 36 hours. Most of the men of the town had been killed or taken prisoner. The displaced women and children moved into the basements and attics of their neighbors' homes.

While we unloaded, a group of children sat on a wall and watched. We exchanged cordial, "Wie geht es Ihnens?" and smiles as we passed back and forth. Among the group was an adorable, alert four-year-old boy who reminded me of pictures of myself at that age. After we finished with work, I scouted around and found candy and chewing gum for our faithful audience.

I pointed to myself and spoke my name. Then, I pointed to each one to respond with his or her name. The first to comprehend the name game was Siegfried, my doppelganger. I listened to the names of all the boys and girls and rewarded each. Then I tossed Siegfried up into the air and rode him on my shoulders to our chow line. I shared my mess kit and hot chocolate with him. We became fast friends.

During our stay in Gmuend, Siegfried joined me on every chow line. He was fascinated by the variety of foods. When I tried to explain that Florida was my home, by describing oranges and lemons, he was completely baffled. He had never seen citrus fruit. We were not supposed to fraternize with the enemy, but I felt it was important to demonstrate to the German children that Americans were friendly people, not grudge-bearing victors. I secretly spoke to Siegfried's mother and sister, Frau Maria Hepperle and Irena, over the fence. She told me that her husband had been killed on the Russian front.

After lunch on our second day in Gmuend, I lined the children up in front of our house and played the name game a second time. Siegfried was at the end of the line. When I got to him, I had already distributed all the candy in the bag. When I turned to go back inside, Siegfried's lower lip trembled as he contemplated being left out. When I reached the door, I called, "Hey, kid, come here." He ran to me and I presented the Hershey bar I had saved for him. His sparkling eyes told me that he saw humor in the way I surprised him. Late that evening just at dusk, I heard Seigfried calling my name out in the yard. I looked out the window. He held up a bowl for me to see. I went out and he presented me with strawberries which he had picked from his mother's garden. He beamed with pride at his rich gift. I hugged and kissed him. I walked Siegfried home to thank his mother.

Frau Hepperle gave me their address. I gave her a picture for them to remember me by and a copy of the May, 1945 issue of *Special Services Topics*, which had a half-page picture of me on stage with other members of the cast of *For Free*. She told me that she thought it best not to tell Siegfried that I was leaving the next day. I understood.

At daybreak the next morning, our company crossed the border into France.

CHAPTER 43

We sped across France in two days to Camp Lucky Strike on the coast not far from where we had landed a long, nine months before. In less than 24 hours, we were aboard the USS Lejeune and at sea in splendid weather on a calm ocean. Each man had his own bunk. By the end of the second day, we were like a happy family on a holiday cruise. We played cards, sunbathed and chewed the fat with the crew when they weren't busy. We told war stories and jokes. We talked about dreams of home. We held great debates about which areas of America were best and about where the greatest opportunities for the good life would be after the war. We read and we listened to music on the ship's P.A. system. At night after chow, our projectionists showed films in the dining rooms. We gave stage performances for the ship's personnel. As emcee, I explained that they were seeing the best of the two revues we had performed for more than a million Allied troops during our overseas tour of duty.

Eddie and I met several sailors who we sensed were gay, but we never had an opportunity to make contact. At one point a hooty seaman called Circus subtly let me know that he was interested in some action. He and his family were trapeze artists. The day before we were scheduled to dock in New York, Circus approached us on deck. "Okay, men. It's set for tonight during the movie."

"What's set?" I asked.

"Us. The Chief Petty Officer, he's real horny. I told him about you. He and I have shared other things before. You'll like him." Then he told us to sit in the back row at the film. He would get us when the time was right.

When the title of the film, *Thrill of a Romance*, flashed on the screen, Eddie whispered, "Prophetic, eh?" Fifteen minutes into the movie, Circus tapped me on the shoulder. We followed him. The Chief Petty

Officer had left his door ajar. His tiny office was barely larger than a clothes closet. The exceptionally handsome officer in his mid-20s was seated at his desk. We squeezed in and closed the door. The Chief stood up. We introduced ourselves and then just stood there. Nobody knew exactly what to say, but we all knew why we were there. Circus broke the ice.

"All right, Eddie. You and the Chief use the top of the desk. Tyler and I will use the floor." And that's exactly what we did. We used every available inch of space in that little room as we switched partners in every possible combination. Before we left, Eddie arranged to rendezvous with Circus and the Chief at the Prince George Hotel two days later. The Chief exited first. Then Circus steered us back to the movie in time for us to see Van Johnson and Esther Williams in a clinch at fade-out.

The New York Harbor was full, so we docked in Boston. Thousands waved, cheered and threw kisses to us. An Army band played pop tunes. The Red Cross volunteers waited for us with coffee, donuts, candy and cigarettes. Everyone on deck waved, whistled and yelled. God, it was glorious! When I sauntered down the gangplank with my duffel bag on my shoulder, I felt as though I had wings on my feet. I loved knowing that I was truly home again and away from war.

We boarded troop trains for Fort Devins, Massachusetts, where we were debriefed and physically checked. The army pampered us like royalty at Fort Devins: steak dinners, all the 3.2 beer you could drink and fabulous desserts. We received our orders. The entire company was given 30-day furloughs before we reported to Camp Lee, Virginia on August 1, 1945. Our orders stated: "Field Training for overseas duty."

Finally, we received official notice. We had heard rumors about a Pacific assignment before we left Austria, but we refused to believe them. We were tired of war. I was tired of the army. Most of the men in our company felt the same. We yearned for peace and civilian life.

Three days after we docked in Boston, we were safely ensconced in Derby's suite at the Prince George Hotel. We swigged pitchers of her marvelous martinis. Even with wartime shortages, Derby managed to serve only the best. I always suspected that her "poor-little-rich-girl" mentality allowed her to shop on the black market with a clear conscience, but I never asked. We told Derby and Edie about the places we'd been and the things we'd seen.

Circus and the Chief showed up on schedule, but we were a day late. We were disappointed to have missed them, but we were never surprised when plans made during wartime went awry.

We limited our New York visit to two days. We needed to visit our families in Florida and Missouri before we returned to the Great White Way to celebrate my 30th birthday on July 27. Eddie called the Army Air Corps to see whether we could hitch a ride on a military flight to Florida. They offered a flight to Orlando on a B-17 that same afternoon.

The B-17 had four propellers, which required two men teams on each prop to get them turned over and spinning. After my partner and I swung down on number one and got it spinning, I raised my head just as number two turned over. Except for the fraction of an inch, I was nearly decapitated. The propeller cut into my scalp. It knocked the hell out of me. I saw stars. I felt like the top of my head was resting in my lower jaw. An ambulance rushed me to the dispensary. The army doctor looked at me. He told the pilot that he could patch me up in a matter of minutes, but he said that I should stay in the hospital at least 24 hours for observation.

"No, doctor, please." I insisted that I was all right. "Just fix me up and let me get on the flight. I haven't been home in over two years." A nurse shaved my head. The doctor stitched the wound and bandaged it. We were off. We joined a young lieutenant in the cargo hold. He recognized us. He had seen a performance of *Stars Without Garters* in England prior to D-Day. Eddie retrieved a bottle of schnapps from his duffel bag. I forgot my headache. Within the hour, the three of us were flying high and swinging on each other as we soared over the eastern seaboard of the United States.

After a week in Florida with my family, we took a train to Missouri for a week with Eddie's family. It was wonderful to be with so many loved ones, but we felt depressed when they asked us about our next assignment. We wanted to tell them that Japan was probably our eventual destination, but protocol only allowed us to say that our next post was Camp Lee, Virginia.

CHAPTER 44

Derby threw a fabulous birthday bash for me. Marie LeBrun, her friend and producer Gilbert Miller's personal secretary, co-hosted. Derby engaged the suite across the hall, but even in two apartments the several hundred guests who swanned in and out between five and eleven were packed like sardines. A succession of musicians and singers provided live entertainment. It was a great big love fest. Wow, wee, woo and Mommy Moo, too!

Helen Luca arrived on the arm of a marine. Wispy, little Helen told me that her priest had advised her to accept Poppy's death and go on with her life. "And that's what I'm trying to do," she said. We were happy that she was making a genuine effort to recover.

Edie was jubilant. She had just received notice that her husband, who had been missing-in-action since the Battle at Iwo Jima in February, was hospitalized in Hawaii and would be home soon.

At eleven when the theatres let out, a whole new crowd of employed thespians arrived to frolic. As Noel Coward said, "I've been to a mahvelous party." Our hostesses bit the dust at 2:00 a.m., but the party went on until five when Eddie, a sailor, a marine and I were the last guests. We decided to continue the celebration at a new, gay after-hours club on East 47th Street. We hitched a ride on the back of a coal truck going up Fifth Avenue. The sailor had to report for duty, so we had a farewell drink with him before he left for Brooklyn. The marine, Eddie and I returned to the hotel and passed out.

Sometime during the early morning hours, we heard a lot of racket out on the streets, but, my God, we were so far gone that Armageddon and Gabriel's trumpets combined couldn't have fully awakened us. We joined Derby for Bloody Marys at noon. She explained that an Army Air Corps plane had slammed into the top of the Empire State Building, just six blocks away. A few minutes after eight, the front desk called

Derby to announce the accident. Then Marie called Derby. "Derby, honey, how are you?"

"Fine. How are you?"

"Oh, Derby, I'm so hung over," Marie said. "Can you believe the noise in this city?"

"Marie, an army plane hit the Empire State Building."

"Is that what that was? Oh, my God, I thought it must be another group of late guests arriving for Tyler's party."

Rodney Hale, a director who attended the party, offered me the guest spot on a radio show at WNEW. Joe Bolton, host of "Fellow on a Furlough," introduced me to two writers who tailored a script to fit my service record. The first-class production featured the Parmalee Orchestra with pianist Frankie Froeba and vocalist Judy Lang. After a full-cast rehearsal, the program was broadcast live at 3:00 p.m. on Sunday, July 29, 1945. I was paid ten dollars and four tickets to *Hats Off To Ice*, which Eddie, Derby, the marine and I enjoyed at the "air-cooled" Center Theatre.

We caught a late train at Penn Station to Richmond. The marine, who had been hanging out with us since several days before the party, decided as a farewell gesture to ride with us as far as Newark. He and I were in the men's room expressing fond adieus when the train stopped, and we missed the conductor's call. He got off at the next station, a local stop, where he had a long wait. He waved and smiled happily when our train pulled out and left him there alone on the dark platform. I guess he figured it was no big deal because he'd been to a "mahvelous party."

On our first day at Camp Lee, the company was re-organized. Eddie was transferred to the 4th platoon. On day two, the entire outfit began extensive combat-training for jungle warfare. Damnation, it was basic training all over again! We marched through swamps. Men and heavy-duty equipment forded rivers. We drilled long hours in the bright, white sun. It was hot as hell in Virginia in August. The mosquitoes in the swamps were as large as healthy honeybees and always on the attack. We nicknamed them "the young B-29s."

We were discouraged. Our six-week training schedule indicated that we would ship out in mid-September. We hated that we would join assault troops slated for the invasion of Japan. We had survived the European fray, and we feared that we might not be so lucky in the Pacific.

Each weekend we were rewarded with 48-hour passes. Larry Matthews, Bucklin's good buddy, lived in Washington. Johnny, Eddie and I caught an early post bus to Richmond on Saturday morning, August 4. We walked to the outskirts of town and hitchhiked to D.C. We were living it up in Larry's spacious apartment at lunch time. That afternoon we went for drinks at the Statler Bar. Wall-to-wall servicemen were laughing, boozing and making contact. Washington was alive with gaiety. Larry hosted a fantastic party that night. Lots of liquor and lots of horny men in uniform. Everyone was uninhibited and wildly celebrating their safe return. We changed lobsters many times and gaily quadrilled.

We returned to Camp Lee in time for reveille on Monday, August 6. We spent all day in the field busting our butts and didn't hear about the attack on Hiroshima until after evening chow when we listened to a transcription of President Truman's speech. "Sixteen hours ago an American airplane dropped one bomb on Hiroshima.... That bomb had more power than 20,000 tons of TNT. It is an atomic bomb...a harnessing of the basic power of the Universe...." It was the beginning of the end. Eighty thousand Japanese had been killed by a single bomb. It was difficult to realize that such a powerful weapon existed. Eddie declared, "Can you imagine what that bastard Hitler would have done to lovely England and three million GIs if he'd had that bomb on D-day? He'd have blown us all to bits." Three days later, the Americans dropped a second A-bomb at Nagasaki. Forty-thousand Japanese were killed. Surely, the Japanese couldn't hold out much longer.

Five of us received notices to report to the Camp Lee Separation Center. A separation counselor told us that we had accumulated enough points to be discharged in four weeks. My extra ten months of service qualified me, but darling Eddie was not eligible for release. Another dilemma.

At 7:00 p.m. on Tuesday, August 14, President Truman announced that Japan had officially accepted the Allied terms for unconditional surrender. August 15 was proclaimed V-J Day. It was all over. Peace at last!

We spent V-J Day, sunup to sunset, on the training field. That night Eddie retrieved a bottle of Italian gin—the last of my Austrian hospital booty—from his duffel bag. Eddie's duffel bag really was the eighth wonder of the world. We got tight as ticks. We were certain that the Pacific assignment would be canceled.

Each weekend we skedaddled to Washington to enjoy all the merriment that we could handle. Each weekday we continued our rigorous training program. Still no official word came through on the Pacific assignment. Finally on September 12, almost a month after V-J Day, orders were issued to prepare for departure to San Diego on September 17. All leaves were canceled. The five of us scheduled for discharge were not included.

I received a physical in preparation for release. The army doctor discovered a small cyst and assigned me to the Post Infirmary for minor surgery. The night before the 34th Special Service Company flew to the West Coast, Eddie visited me in the hospital. I tried to act nonchalant, but my soul ached. I knew Eddie would be safe in a peace-time army, but I dreaded the separation. Eddie was as deflated as a flat tire. He didn't even try to conceal his honest emotions. He let the tears flow. "Now, isn't this a pretty pickle?" he said. I was devastated when he squeezed my hand and left. My worst fear of the past four years had become a reality. I hadn't felt so bereft since the morning I became a soldier. I wept copious tears. Eddie and all the wonderful guys in the 34th were gone.

Bucklin and I consoled ourselves with drink and revelry. We went to Washington. We cruised around the city and met three sailors in Lafayette Park across from the White House. The amiable swabs had a bottle of bourbon in a brown-paper bag. They gave us a snort. We spent an hour shooting the bull. We decided that they were okay, and Johnny invited them to Larry's, where there was always a party in progress. The sailors felt comfortable with Larry's many guests in uniform. They were propositioned by a major and a warrant officer. One of the sailors told the Major, "We came here with those two soldiers. If we fool around, it's gonna be with them." Johnny and I readily responded with abandoned glee. Another happy weekend in the nation's capital, where celebration of peace was the acquisition of several pieces.

I received my honorable discharge three days later. I collected my mustering-out pay, took a bus to Richmond and literally jumped on a train to New York. When I arrived at Penn Station, I called Charles DeMaria who had told me at my birthday party about his great rooming house on East 60th Street and Second Avenue. I moved in that same afternoon.

The next morning I called Marge Morrow, casting director at CBS-Radio. I appeared on "The Jane Froman Show" two days after my release from the army.

I retrieved my stored clothes from Derby's, but my 1941 wardrobe no longer fit. I had gained muscles in the army. For a month or more, I wore my uniforms because it was nearly impossible to purchase new suits due to the demand created by the returning GIs. Whatever the problems, it was wonderful to be a civilian again.

The army finally sorted the red tape. The 34th Special Service Company flew back to Camp Lee a week after my departure. They spent three anxious, tormenting weeks in California before orders came through to disband and discharge all members of the company. Eddie and I were happily reunited in the big bedroom on East 60th Street in late October.

We had survived the war. We had survived the army. The odyssey was completed, and what an adventure it had been.

We were happy. We were optimistic. We were certain that our postwar future together would be the best years of our lives, and indeed they were.

EPILOGUE

The Allies' victory to maintain a free world ennobled my generation, but it did not give me human rights. I still regret that the army and society demanded that I mask my homosexuality. Many of the men with whom we served realized that Eddie Fuller and I shared a unique friendship, but they liked us and accepted us because we worked hard and well. Eddie and I were united by love, but we maintained a facade for people who refused to admit that they knew and liked a queer couple. Our bond provided us with emotional security and stability; the same qualities heterosexuals seek in marriage.

Eddie died in 1979 when a truck hit him while he waited for a bus in mid-town Manhattan. He had enjoyed a 45 year career of performances: Broadway, off-Broadway, national tours, summer stock, dinner theatres, industrials, radio, television and films.

After the war, he appeared on Broadway in *Guys and Dolls*, *I Am A Camera* and *Good As Gold*. He received the best reviews of his career for *The Immortal Husband* in 1968 at the Dublin Theatre Festival in the award-winning USA entry. He performed on numerous national tours: *Auntie Mame*, *The Music Man*, *South Pacific*, *Bells Are Ringing*, *Oklahoma*, *Mame*, *Forty Carats*, *Applause* and *Not Now, Darling*. His film credits included *The Night They Raided Minsky's*, *Bye, Bye Beaverman* and *Dog Day Afternoon*. He appeared in two dozen off-Broadway productions, more than 100 television shows and in numerous dinner theatres across the country. He appeared for ten consecutive summer-stock seasons with the Mt. Holyoke Valley Players. He was a very talented actor and always worked. Eddie would have enjoyed the "full house" at the Actor's Chapel on West 49th Street for his memorial service. Many colleagues spoke words of love and praise for his warmth, wit and talent. He was buried in the Fuller family cemetery in Missouri. I still love and miss him with all my heart.

Derby died of cancer in 1983. She sporadically continued her acting career in stock, off-Broadway and on USO tours until the mid-50s when her family moved to Mexico. All three of her marriages ended in divorce. In Mexico she won acclaim as a hostess and caterer at the renowned Pere Marquette in Acapulco. When Queen Elizabeth visited there in the seventies, Derby was in charge of the arrangements.

I was with Derby the night she died. When a nurse gave her the final morphine injection, she smiled and said, "Oh, Tyler, it's just like a martini." I brought her ashes back from Mexico. She was buried in the Rogers' family cemetery in Connecticut. Jeri Talbott, a talented soprano who appeared with Derby in an overseas USO tour, hosted a magnificent wake. Everyone brought pictures. We looked, laughed and remembered. Derby would have loved the good food, good drink and good conversation. She kept her vow of eternal devotion. I still love and miss her.

Edie died in 1986. She enjoyed a distinguished career in advertising. She received the "Writer of the Year" award from the New York Copy Writer's Association in 1961. Just prior to her death, I spent a happy weekend with Edie at her home in Pennsylvania. She was a forever friend.

After the war I acted on Broadway in *Set My People Free*, *This Time Tomorrow* and *Inside U.S.A.* It was great fun to play opposite Bea Lillie, so I stayed with *Inside U.S.A.* for the national tour. I played five seasons of stock with Eddie at Mt. Holyoke. I appeared on many of the live-drama anthologies of early television such as "Studio One," "The U.S. Steel Hour" and "Kraft Television Theatre." In the fifties, when radio all but disappeared and television moved to Hollywood where the name stars and the large sound-stages were, acting jobs in New York were scarce. I became a director in stock. I liked it so well that I gave up acting. For the next 20 years, I directed and/or produced over 300 shows for Jerome H. Cargill Productions.

Since I retired in 1977, I have worked for human rights causes which seek the liberty that 12 million American men and women in World War II fought to preserve. As a member of a minority group, I never experienced the liberty that I worked for in the army, so as a civilian I have taken up arms again.

I am so proud of the young men and women who have taken legal action against the Pentagon's long-standing policy that homosexuality is "incompatible with military service," and that gay and lesbian personnel in uniform undermine "morale." Hells, bells! Eddie and I did as much or more to boost morale, officially and unofficially, as any members of the Armed Forces in World War II. The military's position lends credence to society's negative attitudes toward homosexuals. Our government's attitude encourages parents to reject their homosexual children. France, Japan and Canada do not ban gays and lesbians from military service. The American gay and lesbian community must insist that "the land of the free and the home of the brave" follow the lead of those advanced-thinking nations.

The hypocritical postures of government and most organized religions toward homosexuals are scurrilous attacks equal to acts of terrorism. They are immoral, illegal acts and unbecoming conduct in a civilized society. In 1980 I divorced myself from the Catholic Church. I did not renounce my faith in God, but I refused to support an institution that perpetrates anti-gay feelings and actions.

My military service provided me with many good memories and a number of life-long, gay and straight friends, especially my German "family"—Siegfried Hepperle, his dear wife Carla and their three handsome sons.

I am not "khaki-wacky" nostalgic; however, I do recall the war years and the people I knew with affection. On Armed Forces Day, Saturday, May 18, 1985, I was the keynote speaker at the dedication of the 1209th CASU permanent exhibit at the Fort Drum Historical Museum (nee Pine Camp). Alfred Marggraf, "Cheers From the Camps" band member, organized the dedication. The fond recollections, the genuine affection and the feelings of contribution made us remember how much we gave to many at a time in our nation's history when gifts of laughter and music were appreciated. The photographs of Eddie, Derby, Poppy, Kimo Dennis, Lenny Kane and others sealed in Plexiglas at Fort Drum are appropriate historical reminders of that unique era.

On June 6, 1994 I did a three-minute spot on WQEW-Radio as a gay veteran to announce that Eddie and I were on the beach at Weymouth doling out books, newspapers and decks of cards when the boys shipped out on D-Day 50 years before. Of the many touching tributes memorializing the heroes of D-Day, I wept when one veteran told about his approach on bloody Omaha Beach. As he ran from the landing craft, he tripped over the body of a young GI who clutched a copy of *Our Hearts Were Young and Gay* by Cornelia Otis Skinner and Emily Kimbrough. I realized that one of the men in our company, perhaps Eddie or me, gave that book to the dead boy. And I marched with pride from the United Nations to Central Park in the 1994 Stonewall Anniversary Celebration. I cannot express the joy I felt at being among thousands of proud, out-of-the-closet gays and lesbians. I must remember to tell Eddie.

> Write about us they (GIs) said a little sadly,
> and write about them I will.
>
> Gertrude Stein
> *Wars I Have Seen* (1945)

SCRAPBOOK

Pictured (clockwise from upper left) Derby Rogers, Tyler Carpenter, Anthony (Poppy) LaPolla & Helen Luca, Eddie Fuller.

STATESIDE

Pictured (clockwise from upper left) Ty and Eddie with Mrs. Fuller, Ty & Derby in "Petticoat Fever" at Pine Camp (now Ft. Drum, NY), Entertainment squad of Pine Camp Theatre Workshop on Maneuvers (all 1942).

"STARS WITHOUT GARTERS"

"Stars Without Garters" helped boost the morale of the U.S. and Allied Forces during the invasion of France. Shown here are the cast and orchestra of the 34th Special Service Company, Morris "Rosie" Rosenberg doing an impersonation of Bette Davis singing "They're Either Too Young or Too Old"(look at those shoes), (bottom right) Eddie and Ty in a skit "If Men Played Cards the Way Women Do."

FRANCE

Second Platoon of the 34th Special Service Company (somewhere in France, Oct. 1944), Posing on a captured German tank (Suippe, France, Dec. 1944), Ty and pals in front of L'Arc de Triomphe (Jan. 1945).